Library Basics Series

1. *Learn Library of Congress Classification,* Helena Dittmann and Jane Hardy, 2000
2. *Learn Dewey Decimal Classification (Edition 21),* Mary Mortimer, 2000
3. *Learn Descriptive Cataloging,* Mary Mortimer, 2000
4. *Learn LC Subject Access,* Jacki Ganendran, 2000

Learn Descriptive Cataloging

Mary Mortimer

Library Basics, No. 3

The Scarecrow Press, Inc.
Lanham, Maryland, and London
in cooperation with
DocMatrix Pty Ltd, Canberra, Australia
2000

SCARECROW PRESS, INC.

Published in the United States of America
by Scarecrow Press, Inc.
4720 Boston Way, Lanham, Maryland 20706
http://www.scarecrowpress.com

4 Pleydell Gardens, Folkestone
Kent CT20 2DN, England

Design by Andrew Rankine Design Associates pty ltd, Canberra, Australia

British Library and National Library of Australia Cataloguing in Publication Information
Available

Library of Congress Cataloging-in-Publication Data
Mortimer, Mary, 1944-
    Learn descriptive cataloging / Mary Mortimer.
        p. cm.
    Includes bibliographical references (p.) and index.
    ISBN 0-8108-3693-9 (alk. paper)
        1. Anglo-American cataloguing rules. 2. Descriptive cataloging–Australia.
    3. Descriptive cataloging–English-speaking countries. 4. MARC formats–
    Australia. 5. MARC formats–English-speaking countries. I. Title.
Z694.15.A56 M67 2000
025.3'2–dc21   99-046644

CONTENTS

PREFACE

This book provides basic instruction in descriptive cataloging and the MARC bibliographic format. It includes explanations and exercises, with answers at the back of the book.

These skills are needed by all catalogers, whether professional or paraprofessional. The book is therefore equally suitable for university and college students studying library science, and others who want to know more about cataloging, with a specific goal or as part of their professional development. Since the bibliographic record is the foundation of all the tools used in a library, from catalog to bibliography to online database, it is important for all library staff to be familiar with at least the basics.

The book is designed for use on its own, in a course of study, or together with the interactive multimedia training package *CatSkill,* details of which are available from the publishers.

You may not always agree completely with the answers provided, and it will be useful to check them with a teacher or experienced cataloger. Despite the best endeavors of the creators of cataloging rules to standardize all cataloging procedures, there is often room for more than one approach or application of the rule.

NOTE FOR TEACHERS

All the fundamentals of descriptive cataloging are covered here: using *AACR2,* and coding descriptions and access points into MARC format. There are many examples and exercises, together with answers for self-checking.

Since it is impossible to include sufficient exercises for every student, or examples to address every possible cataloging problem, teachers should supplement the exercises to provide additional practice.

It is also valuable to catalog real items. For reasons of space, photocopies of title pages, etc., are not included. Some examples have also been altered slightly to suit the requirements of particular exercises. It is strongly recommended that beginning catalogers use real items and more realistic representations of items (i.e., photocopies), in addition to those given here.

The examples can also be used to practice full cataloging. MARC codes for classification numbers and subject headings are included, but answers are provided only for descriptive cataloging.

ACKNOWLEDGMENTS

Thanks to Alexis Yeadon and other Australian colleagues and students for their advice.

ABOUT CATSKILL

CatSkill is an interactive multimedia package designed to teach descriptive cataloging in manual and automated environments.

It deals with the creation of the bibliographic record using *Anglo-American cataloguing rules second edition 1998 revision*, and coding it using the *USMARC format for bibliographic data*.

CatSkill is a self-paced learning tool, which allows you to work at your own speed. If you have difficulty with a concept or need more practice, you can review the relevant module or section(s) of a module as often as you wish. If you are already familiar with the content of a module, you may choose to take the pre-test. If you pass the pre-test, you may continue to the next module.

CatSkill keeps track of your progress through the course:
- It records your attempts and success in the test in each module.
- If you register as a student when you log on, it also remembers the page you reached in the module you were working on. The first screen of the module gives you the choice of beginning again or resuming from where you left off.
- If you register as a browser, it keeps your test results, but not a record of the last page you were on.
- If you can't remember which modules you have done, click on **View Results**.

Many educational institutions clean out their network servers daily, so these records will be thrown away. You will want to keep them—otherwise each time you log on, *CatSkill* will treat you as a new user, and this will become irritating. You can do this by copying your records onto a floppy disk. Since network systems vary, you will need to ask your teacher or network administrator for precise instructions.

Points to remember:
- Make sure you have a blank, formatted disk.
- Follow the instructions exactly. It is important that you do not put your disk in too late or take it out too early.

Chapter 1
THE CATALOG
(CatSkill—module 2)

Introduction
The word *catalog* is used in many ways, sometimes with different meanings. The definition in the *Anglo-American cataloguing rules* is:

> A list of library materials contained in a collection, a library, or a group of libraries, arranged according to some definite plan.

Objects of the Catalog
Charles A. Cutter defined the objects of the catalog in his *Rules for a printed dictionary catalogue* (1876):

1.   To enable a person to find a book of which either
       (A)   the author ⎤
       (B)   the title   ⎬ is known
       (C)   the subject ⎦

2.   To show what the library has
       (D)   by a given author
       (E)   on a given subject
       (F)   in a given kind of literature

3.   To assist in the choice of a book
       (G)   as to its edition (bibliographically)
       (H)   as to its character (literary or topical).

This statement was written over a hundred years ago. Have the objects of the catalog changed very much? Have they changed at all? Should we add or subtract any? Which are the most important? Discuss this in a group, or think about these questions yourself.

EXERCISE 1.1
Write in your own words the purpose of the catalog:

Cataloging

Cataloging is the preparation of bibliographic information for catalog records. Catalogers use a set of cataloging tools, which are the agreed international rules and standards.

Cataloging consists of
* descriptive cataloging
* subject cataloging
* classification.

A Catalog Record

Here is a catalog record from an online catalog, with the relevant parts indicated:

CALL NUMBER	Reference collection RF Z1006.S344 1994	} classification
TITLE	New international dictionary of acronyms in library and information science and related fields / Henryk Sawoniak, Maria Witt.	
EDITION	3rd rev. and enl. ed.	
PUBLISHER	Munich : K.G. Saur, 1994.	} descriptive cataloging
DESCRIPT'N	xi, 522 p. ; 25 cm.	
AUTHOR(S)	Sawoniak, Henryk. Witt, Maria.	
SUBJECT	1. Library science–Acronyms. 2. Information science–Acronyms.	} subject cataloging

Descriptive Cataloging

Descriptive cataloging describes an item, identifies access points and formats access points, using the *Anglo-American cataloguing rules* and appropriate name authority files.

Subject Cataloging

Subject cataloging determines subject headings for an item, which represent the subject(s) of the work in words and/or phrases, using *Library of Congress subject headings* or a similar authoritative subject headings list.

Classification

Classification determines a classification number for an item, which represents the subject of the work in a number and/or letters, using *Library of Congress classification, Dewey decimal classification* or a similar authoritative classification scheme, and provides a location for an item in a collection.

Cataloging Networks

There are many cataloging networks within library sectors, regions, countries and internationally. The world's largest cataloging network, OCLC (Online Computer Library Center Inc.), has over 40 million items cataloged, and libraries all over the world share its records.

In addition there are many other specialized networks.

Purposes of Cataloging Rules

1. To provide consistency within a single library
    That is, a description and headings created by one cataloger need to be consistent with a description and headings created by another cataloger or at a different time.

2. To provide consistency between libraries
    In order to share catalog records and thus reduce costs in a centralized or cooperative library system, libraries must use an agreed set of cataloging rules.

3. To reduce time involved in cataloging
    If codes did not exist, catalogers would have to start from scratch with every work they cataloged.

4. To provide ease of use for library users using more than one library
    Cutter states: "The convenience of the public is always to be set before that of the cataloger."

5. To ensure that the purposes of the catalog are achieved
    That is, the catalog must enable users to find what they need efficiently and reliably.

EXERCISE 1.2

Find out the names of some other cataloging networks, and which libraries or types of libraries they include.

The Catalog Is for Users

The purpose of creating and maintaining a catalog is that library users can find what they need efficiently.

Each library must therefore consider its particular users when it constructs its bibliographic records.

EXERCISE 1.3

Here are two very different types of library. Consider the differences between their users, and indicate the implications for creating suitable bibliographic records.

	Our Town Elementary School Library	National Agricultural Library
Describe a typical user		
What information do they need in the description of the item?		
What kinds of access points do they need—i.e., what do they want to be able to look up in the catalog?		
List other types of libraries with the same or similar kinds of users		

Chapter 2
THE BIBLIOGRAPHIC RECORD
(CatSkill—module 3)

Introduction

Library catalogs consist of bibliographic records for the works which make up a collection. The bibliographic record includes a description of the work, containing standardized information such as author(s) and title, publication and distribution details and the physical description of the work. It includes a heading, which tells us the name of the author, title or other information under which the record will be found. It also includes tracing notes, or tracings, which tell us the other headings under which the work will also be found in the catalog.

An Example

This is the heading

Masson, J. M. (Judith M.)

Out of hearing : representing children in court / Judith Masson and Maureen Winn Oakley. - New York : Wiley, 1999. - vi, 245 p. ; 28 cm. - (Wiley series in child protection and policy) Includes bibliographical references and index. ISBN 0 471 98642 9 (alk. paper)

This is the description, or the body of the record

1. Custody of children–United States. 2. Child abuse–Law and legislation–United States. 3. Children as witnesses–United States. 4. Legal assistance to children–United States. I. Winn Oakley, Maureen. II. Title. III. Series: NSPCC/Wiley child protection and policy series.

These are the tracings, which indicate the other headings.

Description

The description contains information from the work itself. The information is taken from various parts of the work.

Out of hearing : representing children in court / Judith Masson and Maureen Winn Oakley. - New York : Wiley, 1999. - vi, 245 p. ; 28 cm. - (Wiley series in child protection and policy) Includes bibliographical references and index. ISBN 0 471 98642 9 (alk. paper)

Access Points

Users find records in the catalog by a person's name, title, series, organization or subject. The name or term a user searches for is called an access point, since it gives the user access to the record. It is also called a heading, since it is written at the top (head) of the record in a card, book or microfiche catalog. Catalogers determine the access points using cataloging rules, with particular attention to what users are likely to look for.

Main Entry Heading

When a catalog record is created, the cataloger decides that one of the access points is the main entry heading. It is usually the first-named author or the title.

Added Entry Headings

Added entry headings (i.e., the other access points) reflect other names—other authors, editors, illustrators, translators, titles, series and organizations—by which a user may look for the record.

Subject Headings

Subject headings are also access points, since many users look for information on a subject without knowing particular authors or titles.

Subject headings are decided in subject cataloging, rather than descriptive cataloging, but they usually form part of the bibliographic record. A catalog record also contains a classification number, so that the user can locate the item.

Subject headings and classification are not dealt with in this book.

Formats of Catalogs

Increasingly library catalogs are automated, i.e., the records are stored on a computer, and clients find their information using a computer.

However, other formats—including card, book, microfiche, computer printout and CD-ROM—are also used. The major alternative, the card catalog, still provides a flexible, user-friendly method of storing and retrieving library records, especially in smaller libraries. Cards can be created by library staff using a word processor or a memory, electric or manual typewriter. Sets of cards are also bought from cataloging agencies or library suppliers.

Standard access points—main entry, added entry and subject headings—were established for card catalogs. In a set of catalog cards, one card is provided for each access point, with the appropriate heading at the top of the card. An extra main entry card is used as a shelf list card.

In computerized catalogs, each access point gives users the same view of the record. Users generally need to search using the correct heading. Users of sophisticated automated catalogs can look up almost any piece of information, or combination of details, to find a record.

EXERCISE 2.1

Here are two online catalog records. Highlight all the access points you would find in an OPAC you are familiar with.

a.

CALL NUMBER	RF 020.148 S729
TITLE	New international dictionary of acronyms in library and information science and related fields / Henryk Sawoniak, Maria Witt.
EDITION	3rd rev. and enl. ed.
PUBLISHER	Munich : K.G. Saur, 1994.
ISBN/ISSN	3598111711
DESCRIPT'N	xi, 522 p. ; 25 cm.
AUTHOR(S)	Sawoniak, Henryk. Witt, Maria.
SUBJECT	1. Library science–Acronyms. 2. Information science–Acronyms.

b.

CALL NUMBER	AS36 .R3 R-2250
TITLE	The economic potential of the Arab countries : prepared for Director of Net Assessment, Office of the Secretary of Defense / Arthur Smithies.
AUTHOR	Smithies, Arthur.
ADD AUTHOR	United States. Dept. of Defense. Director of Net Assessment.
PUBLISHER	Santa Monica, Calif. : Rand, 1978.
ISBN/ISSN	0833000594
PHYS DESCR	xiii, 93 p. ; 28 cm.
SERIES	Rand report ; R-2250-NA.
SUBJECT	Economic forecasting–Arab countries. Arab countries–Economic conditions.
NOTE	Includes bibliographical references.

Chapter 3
INTERNATIONAL STANDARD BIBLIOGRAPHIC DESCRIPTION
(CatSkill—module 4)

Introduction

The International Standard Bibliographic Description (ISBD) was developed by the International Federation of Library Associations and Institutions (IFLA), to provide a standardized way of describing items being cataloged. A general framework for ISBDs—called ISBD (G)—was agreed upon by IFLA in the early 1970s and published in 1977.

The description used in the *Anglo-American cataloguing rules second edition (AACR2)* is based on ISBD (G).

Specific types of materials are described using ISBDs which are based on the ISBD (G). They include:

ISBD (M) (Monographs) 1978 (revised edition)

ISBD (S) (Serials) 1977

ISBD (G) (General) 1978 [The framework document]

ISBD (CM) (Cartographic Materials) 1977

ISBD (NBM) (Non-book Materials) 1977

ISBD (A) (Antiquarian) 1980

ISBD (PM) (Printed Music) 1980

ISBD (CP) (Component Parts) 1988

ISBD (CF) (Computer Files) 1989

Areas of Description

The description is divided into the following eight areas:

- Title and statement of responsibility
- Edition
- Material (or type of publication) specific details
- Publication, distribution, etc.
- Physical description
- Series
- Note
- Standard number and terms of availability.

Some items require all areas of description. Most items do not need all eight areas; then the description includes only the appropriate areas.

Elements

Each area of the description contains a number of elements. The rules in *AACR2* Part I describe the elements of each area in detail.

Punctuation

Punctuation is used in the ISBD
- to show the beginning of each area
- to separate the elements within each area
- to identify particular elements by the punctuation that precedes them.

Punctuation precedes (or comes before) each area or element within an area. Thus, size is always preceded by a semicolon (;), whatever else is in the physical description.

e.g.,   xi, 309 p. : ill. ; **23 cm.**
          665p. ; **21 cm.**

EXERCISE 3.1

Write out each of the following bibliographical records using ISBD arrangement. Begin each note and the ISBN on a new line. Retain the punctuation supplied. Remember that punctuation precedes each element and area.

a.

Title proper	Design & details
Pagination	. - 88 p.
Date	, 1998
Height	; 25 cm.
Place of publication	- New York
Illustration	: col. ill.
Statement of responsibility	/ Candie Frankel, Michael Litchfield, Candace Ord Manroe
ISBN	ISBN 1567996361.
Publisher	: MetroBooks
Other title information	: creative ideas for styling your home
Edition	. - Abridged ed.
Note	Includes index.

b.

First statement of responsibility	/ Izaak Walton
Publication, distribution, etc.	- London : printed for R. Marriot, 1668
Title	The compleat angler, or, The contemplative man's recreation
Physical description	. - [16], 255 p. : ill. ; 15 cm.
Edition	. - 4th ed., much enl.
Note	Dedication signed: Iz. Wa.

c.

Date of publication	, 1995
ISBN	ISBN 0 8386 3572 5.
Pagination	. - v, 257 p.
Title proper	Maria de Zayas
Publisher	: Fairleigh Dickinson University Press
Statement of responsibility	/ edited by Amy R. Williamsen and Judith A. Whitenack
Size	; 24 cm.
Note	Includes bibliographical references and index.
Other title information	: the dynamics of discourse
Place of publication	. - Madison

d.

Note	Includes bibliographical references and index.
Series	- (American Psychopathological Association series)
Illustration	: ill.
Statement of responsibility	/ edited by Elliot S. Gershon and C. Robert Cloninger
ISBN	ISBN 0 880 48951 0.
Title proper	Genetic approaches to mental disorders
Publisher	: American Psychiatric Press
Size	; 24 cm.
Edition	. - 1st ed.
Place of publication	- Washington, D.C.
Pagination	. - xix, 376 p.
Date of publication	, 1994

Punctuation Marks

Here is a list of punctuation marks used in ISBD, and the names used by *AACR2*.

.	full stop
,	comma
:	colon
;	semicolon
-	hyphen
——	dash
/	(diagonal) slash
[ ]	square brackets
( )	parentheses
...	marks of omission (NB only 3 dots)
?	question mark
=	equals sign
+	plus sign

Punctuation Rules

Punctuation in ISBDs is standardized. The following are general rules to be used as a guide:

1. Each area is separated by a period, space, dash, space or a new line; notes are often given separate paragraphs for readability. Although *AACR2* does not specify punctuation at the end of an area when it is not immediately followed by another area (e.g., notes, ISBN), it is common practice to use a period (if there is no other punctuation mark).

   > Title and statement of responsibility area. - Edition area. - Material specific details area. - Publication, distribution, etc., area. - Physical description area. - (Series area)
   > Note area.
   > Note area.
   > ISBN and terms of availability area.

2. Square brackets indicate information which has been taken from outside the "preferred sources" for cataloging.

3. Three periods indicate omissions:
   > "An almanack for the year of Our Lord ... containing an account of the astronomical and other phenomena and a vast amount of information ... of the various nations of the world."

4. Parentheses ( ) are used for different purposes in different areas.

5. Each area uses its own punctuation symbols to identify the elements within the area. The rules for punctuation are given in Rule 1.0C of *AACR2* and at the beginning of each section in each chapter.

ISBD Outline for a Monograph

> Title proper = parallel title : other title information / first statement of responsibility ; each subsequent statement of responsibility. - Edition statement / statement of responsibility relating to the edition. - Place of publication : publisher, date of publication. - Pagination : illustration ; dimensions + accompanying material. - (Series)
> Note.
> Note.
> ISBN : price (qualification).

EXERCISE 3.2

Insert the correct punctuation in the following entries. Use the model above to identify the punctuation needed to precede each element.

a.
Soft paths   how to enjoy the wilderness without harming it   Bruce Hampton and David Cole   edited by Molly Absolon and Tom Reed   line drawings by Denise Casey   Rev. and updated   Mechanicsburg, PA   Stackpole Books   c1995   xvii, 222 p.   ill.   21 cm.
Includes bibliographical references (p. 209-220) and index
ISBN 0811730921

b.
International Year of Disabled Persons   the story of the U.S. Council for IYDP   Washington, D.C.   National Organization on Disability   c1983   96 p.   ill.   26 cm.
ISBN 0 961 06280 0 $9.50

c.
The autobiography of a slave   Autobiografia de un esclavo   by Juan Francisco Manzano   introduction and modernized Spanish version by Ivan A. Schulman   translated by Evelyn Picon Garfield   Bilingual ed.   Detroit   Wayne State University Press   c1996   135 p.   ill.   23 cm.   Latin American literature and culture series
Includes bibliographical references
ISBN 0814325378 (alk. paper)   ISBN 0814325386 (pbk. : alk. paper)

EXERCISE 3.3

Identify particular pieces of information in the following descriptions:

a.
Floortje Bellefleur vindt een poes / Cok Grashoff ; ill. door Lies Veenhoven. - 9e dr. - Alkmaar : Kluitman, 1981. - 92 p. : ill. ; 20 cm. - (Ons genoegen)
Leeftijd tot 9 jaar.
ISBN 90-206-7061-1 : f.4.40.

Floortje Bellefleur vindt een poes
Cok Grashoff
ill. door Lies Veenhoven
9e dr.
Alkmaar
Kluitman
1981
92 p.
ill.
20 cm.
Ons genoegen
Leeftijd tot 9 jaar
ISBN 90-206-7061-1
: f.4.40

b.
Pjesme kroz zivot i bajke za djecu /autor svih stihova u ovoj knjizi, pjesama, crteza i fotografija je isto umjetnica Depcinski Veronika. - Prvo izdanje. - Sydney : Depcinski, 1983. - 15 p. : ill. ; 25 cm.
Cover title.
ISBN 0 9588754 0 5 : $6.50 Aust.

Pjesme kroz zivot i bajke za djecu
autor svih stihova u ovoj knjizi, pjesama, crteza i fotografija je isto umjetnica Depcinski Veronika
Prvo izdanje
Sydney
Depcinski
1983
15 p.
ill.
25 cm.
Cover title
ISBN 0 9588754 0 5
$6.50 Aust.

Levels of Description
The rules allow for three levels of description, with different degrees of detail at each level.

The choice of level depends on the detail required by a particular library or cataloging agency, based on "the purpose of the catalog or catalogs for which the entry is constructed"—*AACR2* Rule 1.0D.

For each level, the description should include at least the elements given in the following illustrations:

First level of description:
> Title proper / first statement of responsibility, if different from main entry heading in form or number or if there is no main entry heading. - Edition statement. - Material (or type of publication) specific details. - First publisher, etc., date of publication, etc. - Extent of item. - Note(s). - Standard number

Second level of description:
> Title proper [general material designation] = Parallel title : other title information / first statement of responsibility ; each subsequent statement of responsibility. - Edition statement / first statement of responsibility relating to the edition. - Material (or type of publication) specific details. - First place of publication, etc. : first publisher, etc., date of publication, etc. - Extent of item : other physical details ; dimensions. - (Title proper of series / statement of responsibility relating to series, ISSN of series ; numbering within the series. Title of subseries, ISSN of subseries ; numbering within subseries). - Note(s). - Standard number

Third level of description:
> Include all elements set out in the *AACR2* rules that are applicable to the item being described.

For an example, see Chapter 4, page 24.

Chapter 4
ANGLO-AMERICAN CATALOGUING RULES
SECOND EDITION 1998 REVISION (AACR2R)
(CatSkill—module 5)

Introduction

Anglo-American cataloguing rules were first published in 1967 in two editions—British and American. It was the first significant international attempt to standardize descriptive cataloging rules, to facilitate sharing and exchange of catalog records both nationally and internationally.

In 1978 the second edition of *AACR* was published. It harmonized the separate British and American texts. Important changes were made, including some which had already been agreed to, and others proposed by users of the rules. Many of these were prompted by the growing automation of cataloging in libraries.

In 1988 *AACR2* was revised, but not enough for the editors to call it a third edition. It was therefore called *Anglo-American Cataloguing Rules Second Edition 1988 Revision.*

In 1993 a set of amendments was published separately. Between 1992 and 1996 other revisions were approved but not published. All these (mainly minor) amendments are now incorporated into *Anglo-American Cataloguing Rules Second Edition 1998 Revision.* The revised second edition is sometimes abbreviated to *AACR2R*, but this book uses the more usual abbreviation *AACR2*. Either revision may be used with this workbook.

Structure

The rules are divided into two parts.

Part I deals with the description of the item being cataloged.

Part II deals with the headings (or access points) which are used to find the item in the catalog, and the references to those headings.

In both parts the rules proceed from the general to the specific.

Part I—Description of Different Materials

The rules for description of specific types of material are closely based on the general rules for description—ISBD (G).

The basic rules for description of all library materials are given in Part I, Chapter 1. The other chapters in Part I contain the rules for describing specific types of material, e.g., books, maps, sound recordings, graphic materials. The types of material covered by each chapter are listed in the first rule of the chapter, Rules 2.0A1, 3.0A1, 4.0A1 and so on.

So the rules for transcribing the information for any type of material consist of the general rules in Chapter 1 together with the specific rules in the chapter for that material.

Part I—Structure of Chapters

Each chapter in Part I is divided in the same way, using the same numbering style.

Rules are numbered by

chapter.areaELEMENTdetail.

E.g., ⎯⎯⎯⎯⎯ 5.1F2 ⎯⎯⎯⎯⎯

Music Area 1 Statement of resp. (Add a word ... if relationship ... is not clear)

The order of the rules in each chapter follows the order of the areas in the description.

EXERCISE 4.1

Here is a breakdown of the naming of Rule 3.7B9:

3	Chapter 3 : Cartographic materials
.	separation of chapter and rule
3.7	Note area for cartographic materials
3.7B	Notes (how to set out, order, etc.)
3.7B9	Publication, distribution, etc., note for cartographic materials

Write down the breakdown for the following numbers :

a. **6.1F3**

6

6.1

6.1F

6.1F3

b. **7.4F3**

7

7.4

7.4F

7.4F3

c.   **9.5D2**

9

9.5

9.5D

9.5D2

d.   **11.2B5**

11

11.2

11.2B

11.2B5

e.   **3.3D2**

3

3.3

3.3D

3.3D2

f.   **8.6B1**

8

8.6

8.6B

8.6B1

Part I—Mnemonic Structure

The first set of rules in each chapter from chapter 2 to chapter 12 is .0.
(Chapter 1 is a bit different.)

In each chapter dealing with the description of material, these rules provide important general information:

.0A Scope
.0B Sources of information
.0C Punctuation
.0D Levels of details in the description
.0E Language and script of the description
.0F Inaccuracies
.0G Accents and other diacritical marks
.0H Items with several title pages
.0J Description of whole or part (chapter 3 only)

Similarly under each format, the arrangement is consistent within each area.
For example, where .1 is the Title and Statement of Responsibility Area:

.1A Preliminary rule
.1B Title proper
.1C GMD
.1D Parallel titles
.1E Other title information
.1F Statement of responsibility
.1G Items without a collective title

EXERCISE 4.2

Supply rule numbers for the following situations :

a.   date of publication for an atlas

b.   a statement of responsibility for "The Secret Policeman's Ball" on audiocassette

c.   a series title for a monograph

d.   physical description for a set of slides

e.   notes for a computer file

Descriptive Levels of Detail

Rule 1.0D specifies three levels of description. The purpose of the three levels is to allow libraries to provide the depth of description best suited to their users.

The first level could be used for all material in an elementary school or small collection, or on a cataloging network for minimal level records. The second level provides a fuller description and is used by most libraries. The fullest level is that used by national libraries and research collections.

Some of the factors which affect the decision on the fullness of a bibliographic description include
* library priorities
* importance of an item to the collection
* relative value of an item
* volume of incoming material
* availability and experience of staff to process the material
* needs of the user.

An example of first level:

> From welcomed exiles to illegal immigrants. - Rowman & Littlefield, c1996. - xxii, 168 p.
> Includes bibliographical references and index.
> ISBN 0847681483

An example of second level:

> From welcomed exiles to illegal immigrants : Cuban migration to the U.S., 1959-1995 / by Felix Roberto Masud-Piloto. - Lanham, Md. : Rowman & Littlefield, c1996. - xxii, 168 p. ; 24 cm.
> Includes bibliographical references and index.
> ISBN 0847681483 (alk. paper). - ISBN 0847681491 (pbk. : alk. paper)

Third level would include all elements in *AACR2* that are applicable to the item in hand. This usually means much more detailed notes, often referring to the particular item in hand (inscribed by ... , also published in ... , etc.)

Part II
Part II contains the rules for headings, uniform titles and references.

Part II also contains 4 appendices.

Appendices
AACR2 has four appendices:

Appendix A	Capitalization
Appendix B	Abbreviations
Appendix C	Numerals
Appendix D	Glossary

Appendix A
Appendix A lists general rules for all languages which cover initials and acronyms, headings for persons, places and corporate bodies, and uniform titles. It then covers capitalization for each area. A section is then given to each language with English first, and in great depth, followed by other languages in alphabetical order.

EXERCISE 4.3
Use Appendix A to answer the following. Include the rule number(s):

a.   What is capitalized in the physical description area?

b.   Is "president" capitalized in "president of the United States"?

c.   Do I capitalize "tropic of capricorn"?

d.   What about "arabic numbers"?

Appendix B
Appendix B lists abbreviations used in bibliographic records.

EXERCISE 4.4
Use Appendix B to answer the following. Include the rule number(s):

a.   Do I use any abbreviations in the title proper?

b. What is the abbreviation for "miscellaneous"?

c. Can I abbreviate "revised by" in a statement of responsibility?

d. Can I use "rev." for "revised" in an edition?

e. Do I always use "Calif." for "California" whether it is in the title or the imprint?

f. Can I abbreviate "Colorado" in the place of publication "Denver, Colorado"?

g. How do I abbreviate "Colorado River, Arizona" in a note?

h. In the heading "United States. Department of Agriculture" can I abbreviate "United States"?

Appendix C

Appendix C guides us in the use of numerals.

EXERCISE 4.5

Use Appendix C to answer the following. Include the rule number(s):

a. Do I use "John XXIII" or "John 23"?

b. If the item has "IV edition" do I use "IV"?

Appendix D

Appendix D defines a wide range of terms used in *AACR2*. These definitions are very important as the text is often based on these strict definitions.

EXERCISE 4.6

Use Appendix D to look up the following meanings:

a.   Edition

b.   Caption title

c.   Half title

d.   Colophon

e.   Kit

f.   Mixed responsibility

g.   Subtitle

h.   Other title information

i.   Plate

j.   Uniform title

REVISION QUIZ 4.7

Use the following questions to revise your understanding of *AACR2*. You do not need to write down the answers.

a. List the 8 areas of description including the number and name of the area.

b. Using only the contents pages of *AACR2* identify the rule numbers for the following:
   - physical description of a videocassette

   - edition of a map

   - series of a monograph

   - notes for sheet music

   - statement of responsibility for an audio compact disc

   - title of a data CD-ROM

   - general material designation of a poster

c. What rule do you always consult in each chapter (in Part I) in order to clarify what types of materials are covered by that chapter?

d. What are the elements of description? How do they relate to the areas of description?

e. What function does punctuation have in a catalog entry?

f.   What parts of an entry are created using:
  • Part I of AACR2?

  • Dewey Decimal or Library of Congress Classification schedules?

  • Part II of AACR2?

  • Library of Congress Subject Headings?

g.   Some of the physical description rules require you to give the number of leaves and plates in a book. What would you consult if you were unsure about the difference between a leaf, a plate and a page?

Chapter 5
MARC

(CatSkill—module 5)

Introduction

MARC stands for MAchine Readable Cataloging. The description and headings of all items in the catalog are created according to the *Anglo-American cataloguing rules*. Coding into MARC format is simply transcribing the description and headings into a form which a computer system can read and manipulate.

In the 1960s, librarians at the Library of Congress began work on a system for distributing cataloging information in machine-readable form. The Library of Congress, in consultation with other libraries, developed a standard format for recording cataloging information on computer tape. This development, known as MARC, has enabled libraries all over the world to exchange cataloging data with each other.

Although the MARC format was developed to standardize machine-readable bibliographic data, many countries and even some library systems constructed their own versions of MARC.

UNIMARC was created in an attempt to define one international version of the MARC format. Although UNIMARC is widely used, especially in Europe, it has not become the international standard.

Librarians in the United States, Canada and the United Kingdom are now working toward harmonizing their national MARC formats, which may succeed in producing one international standard.

Uses of the MARC Format

The MARC format enables computers to sort and file catalog data for purposes such as
* printing catalog data in a variety of formats such as subject bibliographies
* producing other products such as accessions lists, shelf lists, book and spine labels
* producing different types of catalogs such as microfiche and online public access catalogs
* standardizing a machine-readable format for bibliographic records for exchange of cataloging data among libraries all over the world.

USMARC Manuals

The Network Development and MARC Standards Office of the Library of Congress publishes the manual *USMARC format for bibliographic data* which guides catalogers using USMARC. This manual includes instructions for the coding of cataloging data for monographs, serials and non-book materials according to the USMARC format.

The Library of Congress also publishes *USMARC format for authority data*. It contains specifications for the coding of controlled headings—names, subjects and series. It includes the reference structure and the sources of the headings.

Supporting publications include:
- *USMARC format for classification data*
- *USMARC format for holdings data*
- *USMARC format for community information*
- *USMARC code list for countries*
- *USMARC code list for geographic areas*
- *USMARC code list for languages*
- *USMARC code list for organizations*
- *USMARC code list for relators, sources, description conventions*
- *USMARC specifications for record structure, character sets, and exchange media.*

The MARC Record

A MARC record is composed of three elements:
- the record structure
- the content designation
- the data content of the record.

The record structure is derived from an international standard for the exchange of information on magnetic tape.

The content designation comprises the codes and conventions defined by the MARC format. They identify the data elements within a record and enable the computer to manipulate the data.

The content of the data elements in the catalog record is created using bibliographic standards like *AACR2* and *Library of Congress subject headings*. The content of some other data elements —e.g., the date of the creation of the record—is defined in the MARC format.

Fields and Tags

In a computer system, a record is a collection of related fields.

In a MARC record, a field contains either coded information (e.g., the date of entry onto the system) or bibliographic information (e.g., the physical description or a subject heading).

Each field has an identifying label. This label is called a tag and consists of three digits.

For example, the edition area—now called the edition field—uses the tag 250.

The Record Structure

A MARC record consists of three main components:

- the leader
- the directory
- the variable fields.

The Leader

Here is a MARC record:

```
LEADER 00908nam##2200253#a#4500
001    91039671
008    911120s1992####mau######b####00010#eng##
020       $a0674673778 :$c$14.95
043       $an-us---
050  0    $aPS173.N4$bM67 1992
082  0 0  $a 810.9/8034$220
100  1    $aMorrison, Toni.
245  1 0  $aPlaying in the dark :$bwhiteness and the literary imagination
          /$cToni Morrison.
260       $aCambridge, Mass. :$bHarvard University Press,$c1992.
300       $axiii, 91 p. ;$c22 cm.
440    4  $aThe William E. Massey, Sr. lectures in the history of American
          civilization ;$v1990
504       $aIncludes bibliographical references.
650  0    $aAmerican literature$xWhite authors$xHistory and criticism.
650  0    $aAfro-Americans in literature.
650  0    $aRace in literature.
```

The top line of the record is known as the leader. The leader is the first field of the record. It has 24 characters, including some blanks, shown by the symbol # in this example. It contains information needed by the computer system, like the physical format of the material, the date the record was entered onto the system and so on.

We will not look at the leader in any detail in this book.

Display of the MARC Record

MARC records are displayed using different symbols and conventions, depending on the computer system. Specific differences are referred to later in this chapter.

The Directory

The directory is constructed by the computer from the bibliographic record. It shows which tags are used in the record and where they are. It is not part of the MARC display for catalogers or catalog users. It is used by the programmer and the computer.

Here is part of a record in MARC communications format. It shows the leader, followed immediately by the directory:

```
00908nam__2200253_a_45000010015000000005001700015008004100032010001600073020002
00350008904000120012405000220013608200020001581000020001782450109001982600006500
30730000260037244000340039850000200043265000230045265000370047565000055005120512
65000450056765000410061270000200065370000220067399
```

The Data Content

The data content is divided into variable fields. There are two kinds of variable fields:
- variable control fields
- variable data fields.

The control fields contain coded information that is used in processing machine-readable records. The data fields contain the bibliographic information of the record, i.e., the description, main and added entries, subject headings and the classification or call number.

Variable Fields and Tags

The data is recorded in fields, each of which is identified by a three-character tag. The fields are grouped into blocks according to the first character of the tag. X is used to represent any other character in the tag.

For bibliographic records, the blocks are:

0XX	Variable control fields, identification and classification numbers, etc.
1XX	Main entry
2XX	Titles, edition, imprint
3XX	Physical description
4XX	Series statements
5XX	Notes
6XX	Subject added entries
7XX	Added entries other than subject, series
8XX	Series added entries
9XX	Reserved for local use

Control Fields

Control fields contain coded information that is used in processing machine-readable records. We do not look at the control fields in this book.

Variable Data Fields

Variable data fields contain the bibliographic information we regard as the traditional catalog record.

In the MARC record, they are:

1XX	Main entry
2XX	Titles, edition, imprint
3XX	Physical description
4XX	Series statements
5XX	Notes
6XX	Subject added entries
7XX	Added entries other than subject, series
8XX	Series added entries

Content Designation

Variable data fields use three levels of content designation. Content designators identify and characterize the data elements which make up the MARC record. Tags are the three-character labels used to identify the field. Indicators provide additional information about how to process the data in a field. Subfield codes precede each data element.

Tags

Here is our MARC record. The tags are bolded:

```
LEADER 00908nam##2200253#a#4500
001   91039671
008   911120s1992####mau######b####00010#eng##
020       $a0674673778 :$c$14.95
043       $an-us---
050   0   $aPS173.N4$bM67 1992
082   0 0 $a 810.9/8034$220
100   1   $aMorrison, Toni.
245   1 0 $aPlaying in the dark :$bwhiteness and the literary imagination
          /$cToni Morrison.
260       $aCambridge, Mass. :$bHarvard University Press,$c1992.
300       $axiii, 91 p. ;$c22 cm.
440     4 $aThe William E. Massey, Sr. lectures in the history of American
          civilization ;$v1990
504       $aIncludes bibliographical references.
650   0   $aAmerican literature$xWhite authors$xHistory and criticism.
650   0   $aAfro-Americans in literature.
650   0   $aRace in literature.
```

Indicators

Sometimes we want to tell the computer to do more than just store the information. For example, in the 245 - Title and Statement of Responsibility field, we want to indicate whether or not the title should be an access point in the catalog. We may also want to tell the computer to ignore some characters at the beginning of the title when it files the title.

This is done by the use of two extra characters.
The title field in our record is:

```
245   1 0 $aPlaying in the dark :$bwhiteness and the literary imagination
          /$cToni Morrison.
```

1 tells the computer to make an added entry for the title. Note that there is no special added entry field for the title in a MARC record.

0 shows that there are no characters to be ignored when the title is filed in alphabetical order. So the item will be filed under "P" for "Playing".

In the example
```
245   1 4 $aThe country house :$bclassic style for an elegant home /$cJenny
          Gibbs ; edited by Alison Wormleighton.
```

1 tells the computer to make an added entry for the title.

4 shows that four characters need to be ignored when the title is filed in alphabetical order. So the item will be filed under "c" for "country", not "T", "h", "e" or the space.

In fields where indicators are not needed, they are left blank. The symbol # is sometimes used to represent a blank (e.g., in the MARC codes at the back of this book).

Subfields and Subfield Codes
The data elements within a field are called subfields.

Each subfield is introduced by a subfield code. These codes enable the computer to identify all the pieces of information which make up the record. Thus the system can retrieve any information it needs.

For example, in the publication, distribution field, the place of publication is stored in subfield "a", the publisher in subfield "b" and the date of publication in subfield "c".

"a", "b" and "c" are called data element identifiers.

Delimiters
In *AACR2* format, data elements are separated by standard punctuation. In MARC format, subfields are also separated by symbols called delimiters. In this book, we use the symbol $. Depending on the computer system, the delimiter may be a hash (#), a double dagger (‡), a pipe (|) or another symbol.

The subfield code consists of two characters—the delimiter and the data element identifier (the letter which identifies the particular data element or subfield).

For example, in this publication, distribution field, the subfield codes are bolded:
```
260   $aCambridge, Mass. :$bHarvard University Press,$c1992.
```

Note that the delimiter also takes the place of a space. There is no space between the punctuation mark and the subfield.

Most systems do not display "$a", since it is the default coding for the beginning of a field. Most systems will also not require you to enter it when you enter the bibliographic data. However it is included in this book, so that you understand its presence and meaning.

Variable Data Fields

Fields with tags that do not begin with 00 are variable data fields. They contain the content of the catalog record, as well as some additional information. The cataloging data is bolded.

```
LEADER 00908nam##2200253#a#4500
001    91039671
008    911120s1992####mau######b####00010#eng##
020       $a0674673778  :$c$14.95
043       $an-us---
050    0  $aPS173.N4$bM67  1992
082    0 0 $a  810.9/8034$220
100    1  $aMorrison,  Toni.
245    1 0 $aPlaying  in  the  dark  :$bwhiteness  and  the  literary
          imagination /$cToni  Morrison.
260       $aCambridge,  Mass.  :$bHarvard  University  Press,$c1992.
300       $axiii,  91  p.  ;$c22  cm.
440      4 $aThe  William  E.  Massey,  Sr.  lectures  in  the  history  of
          American  civilization  ;$v1990
504       $aIncludes  bibliographical  references.
650      0 $aAmerican  literature$xWhite  authors$xHistory  and
          criticism.
650      0  $aAfro-Americans  in  literature.
650      0  $aRace  in  literature.
```

Other Characters

Computer systems also use characters to indicate the ends of fields, subfields and records. They let the computer know what information to display and where it belongs, and enable retrieval of information from the correct parts of the record.

Most systems do not display these characters, and catalogers rarely have to deal with them. Below is a "system" view of our MARC record. "¶" indicates the end of each field; "§" indicates the end of the record. Other systems use different characters.

```
DLC¶19911120085440.1¶911120s1992___mau_____00010_eng__¶__‡a___91135393
¶__‡a0674673778__¶00‡aPS173.N4‡b.M67_1992¶00‡a810.9/.8034‡220¶1_‡aMorrison,_
Toni.¶14‡aPlaying_in_the_dark_:‡bwhiteness_and_the_literary_imagination_/
‡cToni_Morrison.¶0_‡aCambridge,_Mass_:‡bHarvard_University_Press,‡cc1992.¶__
‡axiii,_91_p.;‡c_22_cm.¶__‡aIncludes_bibliographical_references.¶_0‡aThe_
William_E._Massey,_Sr._lectures_in_the_history_of_American_civilization,
‡vv1990‡aAmerican_literature_‡xWhite_authors‡xHistory_and_criticism‡aAfro-
Americans_in_literature_‡aRace_in_literature.¶§
```

Codes for the Description and Main and Added Entries

Codes for the description and main and added entries can be found at the back of the book. Look them up as you need them, and apply them to the items you catalog.

Subject Headings

The main MARC codes for subject headings are included at the back of the book. However, coding for subject headings is not treated.

EXERCISE 5.1

Here are the variable data fields of a MARC record. Look carefully at the record, and answer the questions below. Refer to the MARC codes at the back of the book if you need to.

```
020    $a0517189178
050 00 $aTX715.2.S68$bM34 1998
082 00 $a641.5975$221
100 1  $aMcKeon, Elizabeth,$d1962-
245 10 $aFit for a king :$bthe Elvis Presley cookbook /$cElizabeth McKeon, Ralph Gevirtz & Julie Bandy.
260    $aNew York :$bGramercy Books,$c1998.
300    $a206p. : ill. ; 29 cm.
500    $aIncludes index.
650  0 $aCookery, American$xSouthern style.
600 10 $aPresley, Elvis,$d1935-1977.
700 1  $aGevirtz, Ralph,$d1958-
700 1  $aBandy, Julie,$d1956-
```

a. What is the book's title?

b. Who wrote it?

c. Is it illustrated?

d. Does it have an index?

e. What is the ISBN?

f. What is its LC classification number?

g. What is its Dewey number? Which edition of *Dewey decimal classification* was used to classify it?

h. Who is the publisher? When was it published?

i. What is it about?

MARC Bibliographic Format

Here is an extract from the *USMARC bibliographic format:*

---

020   International Standard Book Number (R)

Indicators
Both undefined; each contains a blank

Subfield Codes
$a   International Standard Book Number (NR)
$c   Terms of availability (NR)
$z   Cancelled/invalid ISBN (R)
$6   Linkage (NR)

Field 020 does not end with a period.

The symbol (R) in the heading stands for repeatable, and means that the field can appear more than once in the record. If for example an item has two ISBNs, each ISBN is recorded using a separate 020 tag.

The indicators are undefined. This means that we enter two blanks following the tag.

The subfield for the ISBN is denoted by the subfield code $a, and is shown as (NR). That is, within one 020 field there can only be one subfield for an ISBN. A second ISBN will need a second field with its own tag and subfield code $a.

Note the statement about the punctuation at the end of the field, since some fields always end in a period, some never end in a period, and some end in a period when there is no other punctuation mark at the end of the field.

EXERCISE 5.2

The tag for a personal name added entry is 700. The MARC coding for the field is:
700 1 $aGevirtz, Ralph,$d1958-

Look up the MARC codes for this field.

a.   What does (R) in the heading mean?

b.   What does the first indicator "1" mean?

Chapter 6
AREAS OF DESCRIPTION
(CatSkill—modules 7-14)

Introduction

This chapter introduces each of the areas of description, and provides practice transcribing and coding each area in turn. Examples are taken from monographs, serials and non-book material. We saw in Chapter 4 that the structure of *AACR2* makes it easier to find the rules for a particular element or area in each material-specific chapter.

For example, the rules for Area 5 (Physical Description) are:

General rules	Chapter 1	Rules 1.5A-E
Monographs	Chapter 2	Rules 2.5A-E
Computer files	Chapter 9	Rules 9.5A-E

For each example in this chapter, transcribe and code only the area specified. In chapters 7-9 you will practice creating whole descriptions.

Rules for Description

Chapter 1 is used together with the chapter for the specific material you are describing. For example, in Rule 2.1B. Title proper, the first rule states "Transcribe the title proper as instructed in 1.1B." However, there are more examples of books in Chapter 2 than in Chapter 1, which contains general examples. So you need to use the rules in these two chapters together. Start with Chapter 2, but expect to be referred often to Chapter 1 as well.

This principle applies to each type of material – use Chapter 1 together with the material-specific chapter. Although the General Introduction of *AACR2* advises you not to rely on the examples, it is very helpful to study them, since they are easier to understand than the legalistic wording of the rules.

General Rules

The general rules deal with
- sources of information
- organization of the description
- punctuation
- levels of description
- language of the description
- inaccuracies.

Area 1 : Title and Statement of Responsibility

Main points include:

- For books, the chief source of information for the title and statement of responsibility area is the title page. Chief sources of information for other materials are given at the beginning of each chapter.

- The title proper is the chief name given to an item. An item sometimes has a title and an alternative title, which together constitute the title proper. When an item has a title and the same title in one or more other languages, we call the title(s) in other languages parallel title(s).

- The general material designation (gmd) is inserted after the title proper to indicate the type of material. It is enclosed in square brackets—for example, [music]. The general material designation is optional but it is commonly used by catalogers. General material designations are listed in Rule 1.1C1. American libraries generally use list 2.

- Sometimes, in addition to the title proper, an item has other title information. This usually follows the title proper on the title page. Other title information provides additional meaning to the title proper. It follows the title proper and general material designation.

- The statement of responsibility identifies the person(s) or organization(s) responsible for the intellectual or artistic content of the item. An item can have more than one statement of responsibility. The statement of responsibility is transcribed from the item. A statement of responsibility can include more than one person or body. More than three persons or bodies sharing one level of responsibility are represented by the name of the first and [... et al.].

- Rules for capitalization, abbreviations and punctuation must be applied to the title and statement of responsibility area. Be particularly careful only to capitalize the words specified by the rules.

- In USMARC format, the tag for the title and statement of responsibility area is 245. The first indicator when a title added entry is needed is 1. The first indicator when no title added entry is needed is 0. The second indicator is the number of characters to be ignored when filing. Each subfield is introduced by a subfield code, e.g., $a.

EXERCISE 6.1

Refer to the rules for this area in the appropriate chapters of *AACR2* and to the MARC codes at the back of this book (or use the USMARC manual, if you have access to it). Transcribe and code the title and statement of responsibility for each of the following:

a.   Title page of a book. It will have a title added entry.

```
A DICTIONARY OF INUIT EDUCATION

John McLaren
```

b.   Title page of a book. It will have a title added entry.

```
┌─────────────────────────────────────────────────┐
│                                                   │
│              PAPUA NEW GUINEA                     │
│              A POLITICAL HISTORY                  │
│                                                   │
│                      BY                           │
│   JAMES GRIFFIN • HANK NELSON • STEWART FIRTH     │
│                                                   │
└─────────────────────────────────────────────────┘
```

_____

_____

245 _____

_____

c.   Label of a videocassette. It will have a title added entry. Include the appropriate gmd.

```
┌─────────────────────────────────────────────────┐
│                                                   │
│              STRESS BUSTERS                       │
│                                                   │
│   A dramatic presentation about stress, change,   │
│         lifestyle and communication               │
│                                                   │
│                  Amanda Gore                      │
│      Physiotherapist, Master Practitioner         │
│             Of Neurolinguistics                   │
│                                                   │
└─────────────────────────────────────────────────┘
```

_____

_____

245 _____

_____

d.   Label of a compact disc. It will have a title added entry. Include the appropriate gmd.

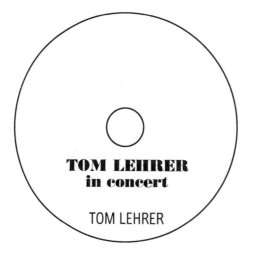

245 _____

_____

e.   Title page of a book. It will have a title main entry.

THE SYMPHONY

VOLUME TWO
Elgar to the Present Day
*
EDITED BY ROBERT SIMPSON

_____

_____

245 _____

_____

Area 2 : Edition

Main points include:
- Information about the edition is taken from the source of information specified for each type of material.
- A new or different edition contains new information, or is in a different format. When an item is reprinted, it does not usually contain new information, and is not called a new edition.
- Computer files usually refer to a new edition as a new version.
- An item which is reissued with minor changes may be a named revision of the edition, e.g., Reprinted with corrections.
- If a person or a body is only responsible for a particular edition, and not for the original item, this is included in the statement of responsibility for the edition.
- Rules for capitalization, abbreviations and punctuation must be applied to this area.

EXERCISE 6.2

Refer to the rules for this area in the appropriate chapters of *AACR2*, and to the MARC codes at the back of this book (or use the USMARC manual, if you have access it). Transcribe and code the edition statement for each of the following:

a.   New Edition

_____

250 _____

b.   Version 6.5

_____

250 _____

c.   Sixth edition. Edited by Jeremy Judson, Sharon Zardetto Aker, Ted Alspach, John Christopher, Michael E. Cohen, Don Crabb, Bart Farkas, Joseph O. Holmes, Ted Landau, Maria Langer, Steve Schwartz, Kathleen Tinkel, and Bob Weibel.

_____

250 _____

d.   First published as *The Potato Guide* 1986. Reprinted 1987, 1988. Revised edition published as *Potatoes : The Complete Guide* 1990. Reprinted 1994.

_____

250 _____

Area 3 : Material Specific Details

Main points include:
* For cartographic materials, the material specific details area is called mathematical data. The prescribed sources of information for this area are the item itself, the container and accompanying material. Mathematical data includes statement of scale, statement of projection, and *optionally*, statement of coordinates and equinox.
* For music, this area contains the musical presentation statement. This indicates the physical presentation of the music (e.g., score, miniature score, score and parts). The musical presentation statement is optional.
* For computer files, this area records the file characteristics. These include the type of file and the number of records and/or statements in the file. Information about the file characteristics is taken from any source.
* For serials, this area records the numeric and/or alphabetic, chronological and other designations. This is very important in serials records. Information about the numeric and/or alphabetic, chronological, or other designation is taken from the first issue where possible. When the first issue is not available, the record should enclose information about the first issue in square brackets, and indicate in a note which issue was used.
* In microforms, the area is used for cartographic materials, music and serials. For example, for the microfiche of a map, we give the mathematical data as we did for a map.
* Rules for capitalization, abbreviations and punctuation must be applied to this area.

EXERCISE 6.3

Refer to the rules for this area in the appropriate chapters of *AACR2*, and to the MARC codes at the back of this book (or use the USMARC manual, if you have access it). Transcribe and code the material specific details area *only* for each of the following:

a.   (A road map of New England) Scale 1:190, 080, 3 miles = 1 inch

_____

_255_____

b.   (Junior baseball monthly) Volume one, number one, January 1964

_____

_362_____

c.   (Ancient historical studies) Fall 1989, Issue one

_____

_362_____

Area 4 : Publication, Distribution, etc.

Main points include:

- Information about the publication details of a book are usually taken from the title page and the verso of the title page. Information about the publication details of a serial is usually taken from the cover, title page, editorial page and/or masthead. Information about the publication details of a non-book item are usually taken from the item itself, its container and accompanying material.
- The elements of this area are given in the order: Place : publisher, date.
- The place of publication is, wherever possible, given as a city, town or suburb. If there is more than one place, give the first named place.
- The publisher is the person or body which prepares and produces the item.
- The date of publication is the date of the edition being cataloged. The copyright date is the year in which copyright was issued in the item. It is usually the same as the date of publication, since items are copyright as soon as they are published.
- Rules for capitalization, abbreviations and punctuation must be applied to this area.

EXERCISE 6.4

Refer to the rules for this area in the appropriate chapters of *AACR2*, and to the MARC codes at the back of this book (or use the USMARC manual, if you have access it). Transcribe and code the publication, distribution area *only* for each of the following:

a.   Title page of a book

Forest Press

A Division of OCLC Online Computer Library Center, Inc.

Albany, New York 1996

260

b.   Label of the audiocassette *California Gold Rush : life in the goldfields in the days of '49* (bought in a Californian folk museum)

Lay of the Land, Copyright 1996

260 _____

c.   Verso of the title page of a book

bf

© 1993 by boyd & fraser publishing company
A Division of South-Western Publishing Company
One Corporate Place • Ferncroft Village
Danvers, Massachusetts

260 _____

d.   Label of a videocassette

© **Prologic Pty Ltd 1985**

Published in association with Longman Cheshire Pty Limited
and Control Data Pty Limited

Unit 6, 663 Main Street,
Mt. Vernon, Virginia 22121

260 _____

Area 5 : Physical Description

Main points include:
*   Information about the physical description of a book or serial can be taken from the whole of the publication.
*   Information about the physical description of a non-book item can be taken from anywhere.
*   The physical description of a book or serial can contain information about volumes or pagination, illustrations, dimensions and accompanying material.
*   The physical description of a non-book item can contain information about extent of the item, other physical details, dimensions and accompanying material.
*   Rules for capitalization, abbreviations and punctuation must be applied to this area.

EXERCISE 6.5

Refer to the rules for this area in the appropriate chapters of *AACR2*, and to the MARC codes at the back of this book (or use the USMARC manual, if you have access to it). Transcribe and code the physical description area for each of the following:

a.   A book is 20.5 cm. high and 14.6 cm. wide, has 287 pages and 163 illustrations including 55 in full color.

300 _____

b.   A continuing serial is 20.3 cm. wide and 24.6 cm. high, the latest issue has 108 pages and a picture on the cover.

300 _____

c.   A computer program has six 3 and 1/2-inch floppy disks, a large reference manual and a quick reference card, contains color animations and sound.

300 _____

d.   A set of 3 digitally recorded, stereo compact discs and a booklet in a cardboard box. The discs are 4 and 3/4 inches in diameter, and play for 56 minutes, 58 minutes and 65 minutes.

300 _____

Area 6 : Series

Main points include:
*   Information about the series can be taken from anywhere in the publication.
*   A series title is usually found on the title page, a separate series title page, or the cover. Some series are numbered. That is, each item in the series has a unique number. A monograph in series can have an individual ISBN and an ISSN for the series.
*   Sometimes a statement of responsibility is added to the series title where it is needed to distinguish one series from another, e.g., Occasional papers, Research reports.
*   Rules for capitalization, abbreviations and punctuation must be applied. Rules for capitalization are the same as for the title and statement of responsibility area.
*   The series statement can contain a series title, a statement of responsibility, a number in the series and an ISSN for the series.
*   The MARC tag for the series depends on whether the series statement is the same as the series heading (i.e., the series access point). MARC coding omits the parentheses.

EXERCISE 6.6

Refer to the rules for this area in the appropriate chapters of *AACR2*, and to the MARC codes at the back of this book (or use the USMARC manual, if you have access it). Transcribe and code the series area *only* for each of the following:

a.   Facing title page of a book. The series heading (access point) will be the same as the series statement.

> *The Peoples of South-East Asia and The Pacific*
> —
> *General Editors*
> Peter Bellwood and Ian Glover

_____

440 _____

b.   Series title page of a book. The series statement will be included in the description, but the series will not have a heading (access point).

> PELICAN BOOKS
> A213
> THE MEANING OF ART
> HERBERT READ

_____

490 _____

c.   Cover of a booklet. The series heading (access point) will be different from the series statement.

Congress of the United States
BACKGROUND PAPER 42

**The Effects of the Tokyo Round of
Multilateral Trade Negotiations
On the U.S. Economy:
An Updated View**

_____

_____

490 _____

_____

d.   Title page of a pamphlet. The series heading (access point) will be different from the series statement. The ISSN for the series is 0404-7821.

Groundwater Research Technical Paper No. 1

Canadian Environmental Assessment Agency
1983

_____

_____

490 _____

_____

Area 7 : Note

Main points include:
- Notes are added to the description to provide useful information which cannot be fitted into other areas. Notes should be brief, clear and understandable. A general outline of notes is given in Chapter 1. Specific applications and examples for different types of material are given in specific chapters.
- Information for a note can be taken from any suitable source.
- Notes are given in the order in which they are treated in the rules.
- Rules for capitalization, abbreviations and punctuation must be applied to this area.
- There are a number of MARC fields for notes, depending on the type of note.

EXERCISE 6.7

Refer to the rules for this area in the appropriate chapters of *AACR2*, and to the MARC codes at the back of this book (or use the USMARC manual, if you have access to it). Transcribe and code the notes area *only* for each of the following:

a.   There are bibliographic references and an index.

_____

_5_____

b.   The cover has the title *Picasso's success and failure* and the title page has the title *The success and failure of Picasso*.

_____

_5_____

c.   A compact disc contains Handel's *Concerto in D minor for trumpet and organ*, Albinoni's *Trumpet concerto in B flat major* and Telemann's *Trumpet concerto in D major* . The Handel concerto takes 10 minutes, the Albinoni 8 minutes and the Telemann 12 minutes.

_____

_____

_____

_5_____

_____

_____

d.   Verso of the title page of a book

> First published as
> *The Potato Guide* 1986
> Reprinted 1987, 1988
> Revised edition published as
> *Potatoes : The Complete Guide* 1990
> Reprinted 1994

_5_____

e.   Masthead of a journal

> **BEDROCK**
>
> BEDROCK is published four times a year
> by Education Impressions ...

_310_____

f.   Cover of a CD-ROM

> Minimum System Requirements
> Windows™ 3.1 or Windows 95, 8 Mb RAM, SVGA Monitor (640 x 480 pixels
> at 256 colors), CD-ROM drive (double speed).

_538_____

Area 8 : Standard Number and Terms of Availability

Main points include:
- Information for this area can be taken from any source.
- The numbers recorded in this area are internationally agreed standard numbers. These are usually International Standard Book Numbers (ISBNs) and International Standard Serial Numbers (ISSNs).
- ISBN is transcribed in *AACR2* format just as it is written on the item. ISBN is transcribed in MARC format without hyphens or spaces. The letters ISBN are omitted from the MARC data.
- If an item has more than one ISBN, you may record only the ISBN which relates to the item being described. Optionally, you may transcribe more than one ISBN, and qualify each of them. This is becoming standard practice, so that the same record can be used for different bindings of the same work.
- Two ISBNs are transcribed in one paragraph in *AACR2* format. Two ISBNs are coded with two separate tags in MARC format.
- A serial has an International Standard Serial Number (ISSN). The ISSN is transcribed as it appears on the item. The letters ISSN are omitted from the MARC data. For almost all libraries, both indicators are left blank.
- ISBNs and ISSNs are recorded in this area.
- The terms of availability are the terms on which the item is available. Terms of availability are an optional addition.
- Rules for capitalization, abbreviations and punctuation must be applied to this area.

EXERCISE 6.8

Refer to the rules for this area in the appropriate chapters of *AACR2*, and to the MARC codes at the back of this book (or use the USMARC manual, if you have access to it). Transcribe and code the standard number and terms of availability for each of the following:

a.   ISBN 0 7015 0465 X cased edition
      ISBN 0 7015 0466 8 paperback edition

_____

020 _____

020 _____

b.   ISSN 0002-9769
      Subscription price $60 per year

_____

022 _____

Chapter 7
DESCRIPTION OF MONOGRAPHS
(CatSkill—modules 7-14)

Introduction

The rules in *AACR2* are intended to create consistent records for materials in different formats. There are also differences in cataloging, particularly in describing, different types of material. This book has a chapter each on monographs, serials and non-book materials. By focusing on each of the different formats in turn, you will begin to appreciate the similarities and differences in cataloging different kinds of material.

Rules for Description of Monographs

As we have already seen, Chapter 1 of *AACR2* states the general rules for description. Specific references to and examples of monographs are giving in Chapter 2. So you need to use the rules in these two chapters together. Start with Chapter 2, but expect to be referred often to Chapter 1 as well.

Although the General Introduction of *AACR2* advises you not to rely on the examples, it is very helpful to study them, since they are easier to understand than the legalistic wording of the rules.

EXERCISE 7.1

This chapter contains the information needed to describe a number of monographs. They cover a range of material, but cannot include every feature of every monograph in a library. Get as much practice as you can on different titles, especially if someone can check your descriptions.

Begin by consulting the rules on sources of information. Taking the information from the correct place is your first step.

Work through each area of the description, and, until you become familiar with the most common rules, check *AACR2* frequently. Look up specific rules as you need them, but you can also learn from browsing, especially among the *AACR2* examples.

Areas and Elements of Description – Monographs

Here is a table of the most common elements in each area for monographs. Familiarize yourself with the areas and their elements. Then look for the information you need, rather than finding a mass of information, and not knowing what to include and what to ignore.

AREA OF DESCRIPTION	ELEMENTS INCLUDED IN EACH AREA
1	Title proper Other title information First statement of responsibility Subsequent statements of responsibility
2	Edition statement Statement of responsibility relating to the edition
3	(Not used for monographs)
4	Place of publication Publisher Date of publication
5	Pagination Illustrations Dimensions
6	Series title Statement of responsibility relating to the series ISSN of the series Series numbering
7	Notes (in the order given in *AACR2*)
8	ISBN Terms of availability

MARC Coding

Introduction

Once decisions are made by applying *AACR2* rules, MARC coding consists of identifying the tags, indicators and subfield codes (called content designators), and adding the bibliographic data, including the punctuation, to the record. USMARC needs the punctuation to be entered as part of the coding process.

It is easier to learn descriptive cataloging by transcribing the description manually first, then coding it. In the workplace however, catalogers usually transcribe the data directly into MARC format, and increasingly often key it straight into a computer.

MARC Codes

MARC codes are provided at the back of the book. Refer to them for each content designator and each element until you become familiar with the most common ones.

EXERCISE 7.2

Using your corrected descriptions, code them into MARC format.

Here is an example:

Looking good in print / Roger C. Parker and Patrick Berry. - 4th ed. - Albany, N.Y. : Coriolis Group Books, c1998. - xviii, 285 p. : ill. ; 26 cm.
Includes index.
ISBN 1 56604 856 7.

MARC

020		$a1566048567
245	10	$aLooking good in print /$cRoger C. Parker and Patrick Berry.
250		$a4th ed.
260		$aAlbany, N.Y. :$bCoriolis Group Books,$cc1998.
300		$axviii, 285 p. :$bill. ;$c26 cm.
500		$aIncludes index.

Note

In MARC, the subfield code consists of two parts, the delimiter and the data element identifier, e.g., $a. The subfield code comes before each data element and after the relevant punctuation. There are no spaces between the punctuation, the subfield code and the data.

a.   Title page of a book

THE PORTRAYAL OF ARABS
IN THE AMERICAN MEDIA

Edited by EDMUND GHAREEB

Published by the AMERICAN-ARAB AFFAIRS COUNCIL

Verso of the title page

SPLIT VISION: THE PORTRAYAL OF ARABS
IN THE AMERICAN MEDIA
Edited by Edmund Ghareeb
Copyright © 1983
by the American-Arab Affairs Council, Washington, D.C.

All rights reserved.

Printed in the United States of America

The American-Arab Affairs Council is a nonprofit organization whose
goal is to promote a better understanding between the United States and
the Arab countries through publications and other educational programs.

American-Arab Affairs Council
1730 M Street, N.W., Suite 411
Washington, D.C.

Revised and expanded edition

ISBN 0-943182-00-X
ISBN 0-943182-01-8 (pbk.)

The book has vii preliminary pages, 248 pages of text, a bibliography and index, and is 23 cm. high and 15
cm. wide.

***AACR2* DESCRIPTION**

MARC CODING (MONOGRAPHS)

020 _____

050 _____

082 _____

1 _____

245 _____

_____

250 _____

260 _____

300 _____

4 _____

5 _____

_____

7 _____

8 _____

(This section is extracted from a standard MARC worksheet)

b.   Title page of a book

Wiley Technical Communication Library

DESIGNING AND WRITING ONLINE DOCUMENTATION

Hypermedia for Self-Supporting Products

Second Edition

William Horton

John Wiley & Sons, Inc.
New York • Chichester • Brisbane • Toronto • Singapore

Verso of the title page

This text is printed on acid-free paper.
Copyright © 1994 by William Horton
Published by John Wiley & Son, Inc.
All rights reserved. Published simultaneously in Canada.

Printed in the United States of America

John Wiley & Son, Inc.
Professional, Reference and Trade Group
605 Third Avenue, New York, N.Y. 10158-0012
New York • Chichester • Brisbane • Toronto • Singapore

ISBN 0-471-30635-5.

The book has xxiii preliminary pages, 438 pages of text, an index and black and white illustrations, and is 28 cm. high and 17.5 cm. wide. The series statement is the same as the series added entry.

AACR2 **DESCRIPTION**

MARC CODING (MONOGRAPHS)

020 _____

050 _____

082 _____

1 _____

245

_____

250 _____

260 _____

300 _____

4 _____

5

_____

7 _____

8 _____

(This section is extracted from a standard MARC worksheet)

c.   Facing title page; heading for the series will be the same as the series statement

---

Cataloging & Classification Series

1. *Cataloging & Classification for Library Technicians* by Mary Liu Kao
2. *Technical Services: A Quarter Century of Change* by Linda C. Smith

---

Title page

Cataloging
And Classification
For Library
Technicians

Mary Liu Kao, MLS, MS

The Haworth Press
New York • London

Verso of the title page

© 1995 by The Haworth Press, Inc. Printed in the United States of America.

ISBN 1-56024-345-7 (acid free paper)

The book has xii preliminary pages, 137 pages of text, tables of catalog records and classification numbers, an index and a bibliography on pages 132-133, and is 21.1 cm. high.

***AACR2* DESCRIPTION**

MARC CODING (MONOGRAPHS)

020 _____

050 _____

082 _____

1 _____

245 _____

_____

250 _____

260 _____

300 _____

4 _____

5 _____

_____

7 _____

8 _____

(This section is extracted from a standard MARC worksheet)

d.   Title page of a book

Food and Beverage Management
Third Edition

Bernard Davis, BA, MHCIMA
Andrew Lockwood, Bsc, CertEd, FHCIMA
Sally Stone, BSc

BUTTERWORTH
HEINEMANN

Verso of the title page

Butterworth-Heinemann
Linacre House, Jordan Hill, Oxford OX2 8DP
225 Wildwood Avenue, Woburn MA 01801-2041
A division of Reed Educational and Professional Publishing Ltd

A member of the Reed Elsevier plc group

OXFORD   BOSTON   JOHANNESBURG
MELBOURNE   NEW DELHI   SINGAPORE

First published 1985
Reprinted 1986, 1989, 1990
Second edition 1991
Reprinted 1992, 1993 (twice), 1994, 1995, 1996
Third edition 1998

© Bernard Davis and Sally Stone 1985, 1991
© Bernard Davis, Andrew Lockwood and Sally Stone 1998

Printed and bound in Great Britain

ISBN 0 7506 3286 0

The book has xviii preliminary pages, 392 pages of text, an index and black and white illustrations and diagrams and tables, and is 24.5cm. high and 18.6 cm. wide.

***AACR2* DESCRIPTION**

MARC CODING (MONOGRAPHS)

020 _____

050 _____

082 _____

1 _____

245 _____

_____

250 _____

260 _____

300 _____

4 _____

5 _____

_____

7 _____

8 _____

(This section is extracted from a standard MARC worksheet)

e.   Title page of a book which will have a title main entry

ORGANIZATIONAL
BEHAVIOR

Roberta Kessler
Ph.D., Columbia University

Angelo Gammage
M.B.A., Harvard University

HarperEducational
A Member of the HarperCollins *Publishers* Group

Verso of the title page

Copyright © 1995

HarperEducational*Publishers*
A Member of the HarperCollins*Publishers* Pty. Limited Group

ISBN 0 06 312368 X

Edited by Diana Giese
Book and cover design by Neil Carlyle

Set in 10/13 pt Minion
Printed in the United States

The book has xxix preliminary pages, 416 pages of text, black and white photos, tables, an index and a bibliography, and is 25 cm. high.

***AACR2* DESCRIPTION**

MARC CODING (MONOGRAPHS)

020 _____

050 _____

082 _____

1 _____

245

_____

250 _____

260 _____

300 _____

4 _____

5

_____

7 _____

8 _____

(This section is extracted from a standard MARC worksheet)

f.   Title page of a book. The book will have a title main entry

ESSENTIAL
ComputerConcepts
SECOND EDITION

Gary B. Shelly
Thomas J. Cashman
Gloria A. Waggoner
William C. Waggoner

bf   **SHELLY
CASHMAN
SERIES**

Verso of the title page

   © 1993 by boyd & fraser publishing company
A Division of South-Western Publishing Company
One Corporate Place • Ferncroft Village
Danvers, Massachusetts

All rights reserved

Manufactured in the United States of America

ISBN 0-87709-097-1

The book has 256 pages, black and white and colored illustrations, an index, and is 27.7 cm. high.

***AACR2* DESCRIPTION**

MARC CODING (MONOGRAPHS)

020 _____

050 _____

082 _____

1 _____

245 _____

_____

250 _____

260 _____

300 _____

4 _____

5 _____

_____

7 _____

8 _____

(This section is extracted from a standard MARC worksheet)

g.   Title page

THE OXFORD
COMPANION TO
MUSIC

BY
PERCY A. SCHOLES

TENTH EDITION
REVISED AND RESET
EDITED BY
JOHN OWEN WARD

LONDON
OXFORD UNIVERSITY PRESS

Verso of the title page

Oxford University Press, Ely House, London W.1

GLASGOW NEW YORK TORONTO MELBOURNE WELLINGTON
CAPE TOWN IBADAN NAIROBI DAR ES SALAAM LUSAKA ADDIS ABABA
DELHI BOMBAY CALCUTTA MADRAS KARACHI LAHORE DACCA
KUALA LUMPUR SINGAPORE HONG KONG TOKYO

ISBN 0 19 311306 6

First edition 1938
Ninth edition (reset) 1955
Tenth edition (reset) 1970
Reprinted with corrections 1970, 1972

Printed in Great Britain
At the University Press, Oxford
By Vivian Ridler
Printer to the University

The book has xliii preliminary pages, 1189 pages of text, black and white illustrations including 185 pages of plates, and is 24 cm. high.

AACR2 DESCRIPTION

MARC CODING (MONOGRAPHS)

020 _____

050 _____

082 _____

1 _____

245 _____

_____

250 _____

260 _____

300 _____

4 _____

5 _____

_____

7 _____

8 _____

(This section is extracted from a standard MARC worksheet)

h. Title page of a book which will have a title main entry

5TH EDITION

INSTRUCTIONAL MEDIA AND TECHNOLOGIES FOR LEARNING

ROBERT HEINICH
MICHAEL MOLENDA
JAMES D. RUSSELL
SHARON E. SMALDINO

Merrill,
an imprint of Prentice Hall
Englewood Cliffs, New Jersey   Columbus, Ohio

Verso of the title page

Earlier editions, entitled *Instructional Media and the New Technologies of Instruction,* © 1993, 1989, 1985 by Macmillan Publishing Company; 1982 by John Wiley & Sons, Inc.

© 1996 by Prentice-Hall, Inc.
A Simon & Schuster Company
Englewood Cliffs, New Jersey 07632

All rights reserved.

Printed in the United States of America

ISBN 0-02-353070-7

The book has 358 pages, black and white and colored illustrations, a reading list at the end of each chapter, an index, and is 29.5 cm. high.

***AACR2* DESCRIPTION**

MARC CODING (MONOGRAPHS)

020 _____

050 _____

082 _____

1 _____

245 _____

_____

250 _____

260 _____

300 _____

4 _____

5 _____

_____

7 _____

8 _____

(This section is extracted from a standard MARC worksheet)

i.   Title page of a book which will have a title main entry

Style
MANUAL

FOR AUTHORS,
EDITORS AND PRINTERS

Fifth edition

An AGPS Press publication

Australian Government Publishing Service
Canberra

Verso of the title page

© Commonwealth of Australia

First published 1966
Reprinted with corrections 1968
Second edition 1972
Reprinted with corrections 1974
Reprinted 1974, 1976
Third edition 1978
Reprinted with corrections 1979, 1981
Reprinted 1986, 1987
Fourth edition 1988
Reprinted with corrections 1990, 1992
Fifth edition 1994
Reprinted with corrections 1995
Reprinted with corrections 1996

ISBN 0 644 29770 0 (cased)
ISBN 0 644 29772 9 (pbk.)

Design: David Whitbread and The AGPS Design Studio
Index: Michael Harrington
Produced by the Australian Government Publishing Service

The book has xi preliminary pages, 468 pages of text, black and white and colored photos, graphs, diagrams and tables, an index and a bibliography on pages 428 to 431, and is 22.7 cm. high.

AACR2 DESCRIPTION

MARC CODING (SERIALS)

022 _____

050 _____

082 _____

1 _____

245 _____

_____

260 _____

300 _____

310 _____

362 _____

5 _____

_____

7 _____

8 _____

(This section is extracted from a standard MARC worksheet)

Chapter 8
DESCRIPTION OF SERIALS
(CatSkill—modules 7-14)

Introduction
Much of the description of serials is the same as the description of monographs.

The most important difference is that, when we catalog a serial, we catalog the complete serial —that is, all the issues of the serial. In all other cases we catalog the item in hand.

The Complete Serial
When a serial is cataloged, all the issues are treated as a single item. This changes our approach to three parts of the record in particular:
* the designation
* the date of publication
* the extent of the item.

Designation
This statement in area 3 is essential for serials, since the numbering is shown here. If the serial is still being published, this area gives the designation of the first issue, followed by a hyphen and four spaces, to show that it is still "alive",

e.g., Vol. 1, no. 1 (Jan. 1988)-

If you are not cataloging from the first issue, but have taken the numbering of the first issue from elsewhere (e.g., *Ulrichs International Periodicals Directory, Serials Directory*), use square brackets,

e.g., [Vol. 1, no. 1 (Jan. 1988)]-

Dates of Publication
The dates of publication of a serial are the date of the first issue to the date of the last issue. Until the serial ceases, the date (i.e., year) is also left open by using a hyphen and four spaces,

e.g., 1985-

If you are not cataloging from the first issue, also use square brackets for the date,

e.g., [1985]-

Extent of Item
In the physical description area, the first element for a monograph is the number of pages or volumes. In a serial, we must give the number of volumes in the complete serial. If the serial is still being published, this element will also be left open, since we do not know how many volumes the complete serial will have,

e.g.,   v.

When a Serial Ceases

When a serial ceases, the numbering system and the date of publication are closed off by the numbering and date of the last issue, and the total number of volumes is filled in,

e.g.,   Vol. 1, no. 1 (Jan. 1988)-v. 9, no. 12 (Dec. 1996)

      1988-1996

      9 v.

Notes

Most serial records have one or more notes, including

- frequency (if it is not clear from the title)
- changes in physical format or publication details
- the issue on which the description is based (if the first issue is not available).

Rules for Description of Serials

Chapters 1 and 12 of *AACR2* are used together for describing serials. If a serial is in a form other than print, e.g., a serial videorecording—the chapters dealing with both formats must be consulted, as well as the general rules in Chapter 1.

Change of Title

When a change of title or other major change occurs, a new entry may be created.

An Example of a Serial Description

Area 1 - title and statement of responsibility   Area 3 - material specific details (designation)

The American journal of theology. - Vol. 1, no. 1 (Jan. 1897)-v. 24, no. 4 (Oct. 1920). - Area 4 - publication etc. details

Chicago : University of Chicago Press, 1897-1920.

Area 5 - physical description

24 v. ; 26 cm.

Later title: Journal of religion

Area 7 - notes

Contents: Vols. 2-6 includes "Theological and Semitic literature for 1898-1901 ; a bibliographical supplement to the American journal of theology and the American journal of Semitic languages and literatures".

Indexes: Vols. 1 (1897)-v. 24 (1920) in v. 24, pp. 529-629.

EXERCISE 8.1

Look at each of the following serial records and answer the questions.

1.   Michigan international business studies. – Vol. 1, no. 1-   . – Ann Arbor : Bureau of Business Research, Graduate School of Business Admininstration, Michigan University, 1963-   . –   v. : ill. ; 23 cm.
      Quarterly.

   a.   What is the designation?

   b.   Is the serial still published, or has it ceased?

   c.   What are the date(s) of publication?

   d.   Where is the frequency recorded?

2.   Optometry and vision science : official publication of the American Academy of Optometry. – Vol. 66, no. 1 (Jan. 1989)-   . – Baltimore, Md. : published for the Academy by Williams & Wilkins, 1989- . –   v. : ill. ; 28 cm.
      Monthly.
      Former title: American journal of optometry and physiological optics.
      ISSN 1040-5488.

   a.   What is the designation?

   b.   Why do you think it is not Vol. 1, no. 1 (the first issue)?

EXERCISE 8.2

This chapter contains the information needed to describe a number of serials. They cover a range of material, but cannot include every feature of every serial in a library. Get as much practice as you can on different titles, especially if someone can check your descriptions.

Begin by consulting the rules on sources of information. Taking the information from the correct place is your first step.

Work through each area of the description, and, until you become familiar with the most common rules, check *AACR2* frequently. Look up specific rules as you need them, but you can also learn from browsing, especially among the *AACR2* examples.

EXERCISE 8.3

Using your corrected descriptions, code them into MARC format.

Areas and Elements of Description – Serials

Here is a table of the most common elements in each area for serials. Familiarize yourself with the areas and their elements. Then look for the information you need.

AREA OF DESCRIPTION	ELEMENTS INCLUDED IN EACH AREA
1	Title proper Other title information First statement of responsibility Subsequent statements of responsibility (less frequent for serials)
2	Edition statement Statement of responsibility relating to the edition (unusual for serials)
3	Chronological/numeric designation
4	Place of publication Publisher Date(s) of publication
5	Extent of item (i.e., number of volumes) Illustrations Dimensions
6	Series title Statement of responsibility relating to the series ISSN of the series Series numbering (very unusual for serials)
7	Notes (in the order given in *AACR2*)
8	ISSN Terms of availability

a.   Cover

JANUARY 1970
AMERICAN
LIBRARIES
THE MAGAZINE OF THE AMERICAN LIBRARY ASSOCIATION

Contents page

CONTENTS
AMERICAN LIBRARIES • JANUARY 1970 • VOL. 1. NO. 1 • ISSN 0002-9769

News Fronts

. . . .

Conference Preview

. . . .

Features

. . . .

Masthead

AMERICAN LIBRARIES
50 E. Huron St., Chicago, IL 60611
tel. 312-280-4216; fax 312-440-0901; e-mail american libraries@ala.org
Published monthly except bimonthly June-July by ALA. ISSN 0002-9769. Printed in U.S.A. Subscription price included in ALA dues. Available to libraries on paid subscription: $60 per year, US, Canada. Foreign: $70 per year.

… *American Libraries* is the official organ of the ALA …

ALA encourages publication in the news columns of *American Libraries* of news about all matters of import to libraries and librarians. The editor is guaranteed independence in gathering, reporting, and publishing news according to the principles of the Association's policies on intellectual freedom.

The serial is 27.2 cm. high.

AACR2 **DESCRIPTION**

MARC CODING (SERIALS)

022 _____

050 _____

082 _____

1 _____

245

_____

260 _____

300 _____

310 _____

362 _____

5

_____

7 _____

8 _____

(This section is extracted from a standard MARC worksheet)

b.   Cover

The International Journal
Of Management Science

Pergamon Press Limited

Inside front cover

OMEGA
The International Journal of Management Science
February 1973   Volume 1, Number 1

Chief Editor
Professor Samuel Eilon, DSc (Eng) PhD
Department of Management Science
Imperial College of Science and Technology
Exhibition Road, London SW7 2BX

.....

Annual Subscription Rates
Published bi-monthly. For libraries, university departments,
government laboratories, industrial and other multiple-reader
institutions, £18.00.

.....

Publishing and Advertising Offices
Pergamon Press Ltd., Headington Hill Hall, Oxford OX3 0BW, England
Pergamon Press Ltd., Maxwell House, Fairview Park, Elmsford,
New York 10523, U.S.A.

Copyright © 1973 Pergamon Press Ltd.

This serial has black and white drawings and photographs, and is 23.5 cm. high; ISSN 0305-0483.

AACR2 DESCRIPTION

MARC CODING (SERIALS)

022 _____

050 _____

082 _____

1 _____

245

_____

260 _____

300 _____

310 _____

362 _____

5

_____

7 _____

8 _____

(This section is extracted from a standard MARC worksheet)

c.   Title page

JOURNAL OF CONTEMPORARY AFRICAN STUDIES

VOLUME 1   OCTOBER 1981   NUMBER 1

ARTICLES

....

REVIEW ARTICLE

....

REVIEWS

....

Inside front cover

JOURNAL OF CONTEMPORARY AFRICAN STUDIES

The *Journal of Contemporary African Studies* is an interdisciplinary biannual of research and writing in the human sciences – economics, political science, international affairs...

Responsibility for opinions expressed and for the accuracy of facts published ... rests solely with the individual authors or reviewers.

EDITORS
DENIS VENTER and RICHARD CORNWELL

© Africa Institute of South Africa 1981

Published in April and October of each year by the Africa Institute of South Africa, Pretoria, at an annual subscription of R8,00, single copies R5,00 ...

....

This serial is 23.1 cm. high.

AACR2 DESCRIPTION

MARC CODING (SERIALS)

022 _____

050 _____

082 _____

1 _____

245 _____

_____

260 _____

300 _____

310 _____

362 _____

5 _____

_____

7 _____

8 _____

(This section is extracted from a standard MARC worksheet)

d.   Title page

The Contemporary Pacific

A Journal of Island Affairs

Volume 9 • Number 2

Fall 1997

CENTER FOR PACIFIC ISLANDS STUDIES
&
UNIVERSITY OF HAWAI'I PRESS

Inside front cover

THE CONTEMPORARY PACIFIC is published twice a year, in Spring and Fall ...
Opinions expressed in these pages are the responsibility of the authors.

Verso of the title page

THE CONTEMPORARY PACIFIC is published twice a year, in Spring and Fall ...
Opinions expressed in these pages are the responsibility of the authors.

© 1997 by University of Hawai'i Press. All rights reserved. Manufactured in
the United States of America.

ISSN 1043-898X

This serial is not illustrated, and is 25.2 cm. high. The first issue was Volume 1, number 1, Spring 1989.

AACR2 DESCRIPTION

MARC CODING (SERIALS)

022 _____

050 _____

082 _____

1 _____

245

_____

260 _____

300 _____

310 _____

362 _____

5

_____

7 _____

8 _____

(This section is extracted from a standard MARC worksheet)

e.   Cover

THE UNIVERSITY OF NEWCASTLE
NEW SOUTH WALES

HISTORICAL JOURNAL

Price : 75 cents.   Issue 1, March 1968.

Inside front cover

CONTENTS

The Editorial Committee consists of all the full-time members
of the Department of History, University of Newcastle.

The Editors are not responsible for the opinions of contributors
to the Journal.

This serial was intended to appear annually, and is 21.2 cm. high. This issue has 48 pages.

***AACR2* DESCRIPTION**

MARC CODING (SERIALS)

022 _____

050 _____

082 _____

1 _____

245 _____

_____

260 _____

300 _____

310 _____

362 _____

5 _____

_____

7 _____

8 _____

(This section is extracted from a standard MARC worksheet)

Chapter 9
DESCRIPTION OF NON-BOOK MATERIALS
(CatSkill—modules 7-14)

Introduction
Most of the description of non-book materials is the same as for monographs and serials. The major differences are in the material specific details, physical description and notes.

Material Specific Details
Three types of non-book materials use area 3, the area containing details specific to a particular material type:
- cartographic materials—mathematical data (scale, projection and, optionally, coordinates and equinox)
- printed music—musical presentation statement (optional area)
- computer files—file characteristics (data or program, number of records).

Microform records also use this area if it is part of the original record. For example, a microfilm of a serial includes the designation(s) of the original serial.

Physical Description
The physical description is different for each kind of material. You need to consult the chapter for the particular material type, especially the examples given in *AACR2*.

Notes
Notes are used extensively for many non-book items, to record all the extra information not included in the rest of the description. This includes cast and credits of sound and videorecordings, system requirements of computer software and much other vital data.

EXERCISE 9.1
This chapter contains the information needed to describe a number of non-book items. They cover a range of material, but cannot include every feature of every non-book item in a library. Get as much practice as you can on different titles, especially if someone can check your descriptions.

Begin by consulting the rules on sources of information. Taking the information from the correct place is your first step.

Work through each area of the description, and, until you become familiar with the most common rules, check *AACR2* frequently. Look up specific rules as you need them, but you can also learn from browsing, especially among the *AACR2* examples.

EXERCISE 9.2
Using your corrected descriptions, code them into MARC format.

Areas and Elements of Description—Non-Book Materials

Here is a table of the most common elements in each area for non-book material. Familiarize yourself with the areas and their elements. Then look for the information you need.

AREA OF DESCRIPTION	ELEMENTS INCLUDED IN EACH AREA
1	Title proper GMD Other title information First statement of responsibility Subsequent statements of responsibility
2	Edition statement Statement of responsibility relating to the edition
3	Mathematical data (cartographic materials) Musical presentation statement (printed music) File characteristics (computer files)
4	Place of publication Publisher Date of publication
5	Extent of item Other physical details Dimensions Accompanying material
6	Series title Statement of responsibility relating to the series ISSN of the series Series numbering
7	Notes (in the order given in *AACR2*)
8	ISMN (printed music) Terms of availability

a.   Front cover of an audiocassette slipcase

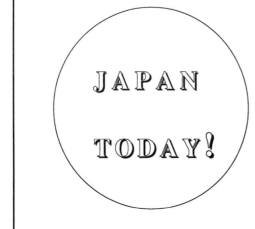

JAPAN
TODAY!

A Westerner's
Guide to the People,
Language and Culture
of Japan

Theodore F. Welch
Hiroki Kato

Accompanying booklet

JAPAN
TODAY!

A Westerner's Guide to the People, Language and
Culture of Japan

THEODORE F. WELCH, Ph.D.   HIROKI KATO, Ph.D.
Northern Illinois University   Northwestern University

PASSPORT BOOKS
Trade Imprint of National Textbook Company
Lincolnwood, Illinois U.S.A.
1991

Back cover of the slipcase

ISBN 0-8442-8503-X

This slipcase contains 1 audiocassette and plays for 56 minutes.

AACR2 DESCRIPTION

MARC CODING (NON-BOOK MATERIAL)

020 _____

050 _____

082 _____

1 _____

245 _____

_____

250 _____

260 _____

300 _____

4 _____

5 _____

_____

7 _____

8 _____

(This section is extracted from a standard MARC worksheet)

b.   Compact disc

Notes in CD case

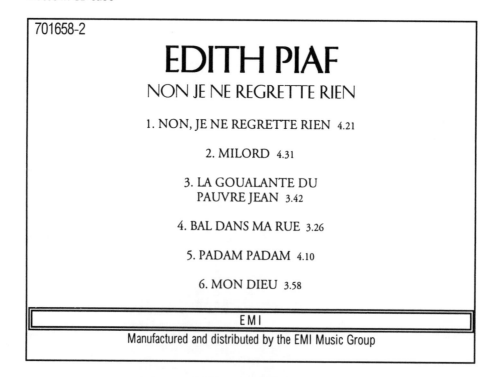

Compact discs are recorded digitally. This disc was bought in Albuquerque, New Mexico.

***AACR2* DESCRIPTION**

MARC CODING (NON-BOOK MATERIAL)

020 _____

050 _____

082 _____

1 _____

245 _____

_____

250 _____

260 _____

300 _____

4 _____

5 _____

_____

7 _____

8 _____

(This section is extracted from a standard MARC worksheet)

c .   Front cover of a map

European Route Planning Series

AA
South East Europe

**Bulgaria • Greece • Hungary
Romania • Yugoslavia**

20 miles to 1 inch   *No. 5*

Back cover of a map

European Route Planning Series

AA European Route Planning Series:

1. France
2. Spain and Portugal
3. Benelux and Germany
4. Austria, Italy and Switzerland
5. South East Europe
6. Scandinavia
7. Great Britain and Ireland

20 miles to 1" scale

Distributed in the United Kingdom by the Publications Division of the Automobile Association, Fanum House, Basingstoke, Hants RG21 2EA, and overseas by the British Tourist Authority, 64 St James Street, London SW1A 1NF.

ISBN 0 86145 072 8

This map is colored, 52 cm. high and 136 cm. wide, and was bought in London in 1986.

AACR2 DESCRIPTION

MARC CODING (NON-BOOK MATERIAL)

020 _____

050 _____

082 _____

1 _____

245 _____

_____

250 _____

260 _____

300 _____

4 _____

5 _____

_____

7 _____

8 _____

(This section is extracted from a standard MARC worksheet)

d.   One of 5 computer diskettes

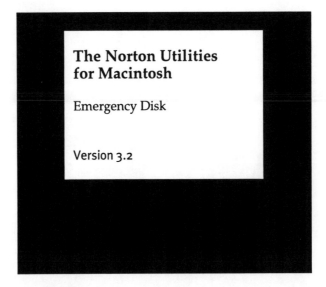

Title page of user manual

Using Norton Utilities
for Macintosh

SYMANTEC.

THE NORTON
UTILITIES

Title page verso of user manual

Norton Utilities for Macintosh

Copyright © 1995 Symantec Corporation.

No part of this publication may be copied without the express written permission of Symantec Corporation, Peter Norton Group, 10201 Torre Avenue, Cupertino, CA 95014.

Printed in Ireland.

AACR2 DESCRIPTION

MARC CODING (NON-BOOK MATERIAL)

020 _____

050 _____

082 _____

1 _____

245 _____

_____

250 _____

260 _____

300 _____

4 _____

5 _____

_____

7 _____

8 _____

(This section is extracted from a standard MARC worksheet)

e.   Cover of a videocassette

CANE TOADS

AN UNNATURAL HISTORY

Written & Directed by Mark Lewis

PG

PARENTAL GUIDANCE RECOMMENDED

A mixture of Comedy, Environmental Tragedy and Scientific History.

Back cover

A Ribberting Experience

....

Australia is being rapidly taken over by a fat slimy ugly creature who
sees its sole purpose in life being the pursuit of sexual gratification.
Bufo Marinus—the cane toad—was imported into Queensland from
Hawaii in 1935 for a specific reason—to combat the grey-back beetle
that was destroying the sugar cane crop.

....

FILM AUSTRALIA

Distributed in Australia by Hoyts/Polygram Video under licence.
© Film Australia 1987. Running time: 46 minutes approx.

This video is 1/2 inch wide, VHS, color and sound, PAL recording system, photographers Jim Frazier and
Wayne Taylor, edited by Lindsay Frazer.

***AACR2* DESCRIPTION**

MARC CODING (NON-BOOK MATERIAL)

020 _____

050 _____

082 _____

1 _____

245

_____

250 _____

260 _____

300 _____

4 _____

5

_____

7 _____

8 _____

(This section is extracted from a standard MARC worksheet)

Chapter 10
ACCESS POINTS
(CatSkill—module 15)

Introduction
An access point is a name or term under which we find a bibliographic record in a catalog. It is also called a heading.

Access points include main and added entry headings. Each record has one main entry heading. All others are added entry headings. A record can have many added entry headings, providing as many access points as library users may need to find the record in the catalog.

Establishing Access Points
In establishing access points, there are two main steps to take:
- selection of access points, one of which will be the main entry heading and others will be added entry headings
- identification of the form of heading to be used in the catalog, listing, bibliography, or visible index.

AACR2—Part II
Part II of *AACR2* gives all the rules for determining these two steps:

Chapter 21 - selecting access points and determining the main entry and added entry headings

Chapter 22 - the form of heading used for personal names

Chapter 23 - the form of heading used for geographic names and place names

Chapter 24 - the form of heading used for corporate bodies

Chapter 25 - whether a uniform title should be added and how to format it

Chapter 26 - the references catalog users need to find the headings chosen by the catalogers.

Intellectual and Artistic Responsibility
In the description of items, we transcribe statements of responsibility which identify persons responsible for the intellectual or artistic content of an item.

If a person writes a book, he or she is responsible for the intellectual content. If a person composes a piece of music, he or she is responsible for the artistic content. Sometimes it is difficult to distinguish between intellectual and artistic content of an item. Fortunately we don't have to, since the rules group them together.

Condition of Authorship

These are the types of responsibility that exist in a work. For each type, *AACR2* has rules to determine main and added entry headings:

- Single personal responsibility
  - personal authorship
  - communication by a person in an official position (official communication)
- Single corporate responsibility
- Multiple personal responsibility
  - shared responsibility
  - mixed responsibility
- Multiple corporate responsibility
  - shared responsibility
  - mixed responsibility
- Collections and works produced under editorial direction
  - with a collective title
  - without a collective title
- Unknown, unnamed, uncertain responsibility
- Wrongly attributed responsibility.

Shared Responsibility

Two or more persons or bodies performing the same function—that is, writing together, editing together, illustrating together and so on—have shared responsibility.

```
COMPENSATING FOR DEVELOPMENT:
THE BOUGAINVILLE CASE

RICHARD BEDFORD and ALEXANDER MAMAK
```

Mixed Responsibility

A work of mixed responsibility is one to which different persons or bodies make intellectual or artistic contributions by performing different functions, e.g., writing, editing, illustrating. For example, if one person writes an item and another person edits or illustrates it, the item is considered to be a work of mixed responsibility.

```
THE EDUCATION OF H*Y*M*A*N  K*A*P*L*A*N

Leo Rosten

Illustrated by C. Keeling
```

Personal Authorship

Rule 21.1A1 states:

> A personal author is the person chiefly responsible for the creation of the intellectual or artistic content of a work.

Rule 21.1A2 states:

> Enter* a work by one or more persons under the heading for the personal author ..., the principal personal author ..., or the probable personal author ...
>
> * (In *AACR2*, enter ... under the heading means that we give the main entry to ...)

So, if a work has a single personal author, the main entry heading is the heading for that person. If a work has two or three personal authors, of whom one is the principal author, the main entry heading is the heading for the principal author.

Two or Three Persons or Bodies

Rule 21.6C1 states:

> If responsibility is shared between two or three persons or bodies and principal responsibility is not attributed to any of them by wording or layout, enter under the heading for the one named first. Make added entries under the headings for the others.

So, if a work has two or three personal authors, none of whom is the principal author, the main entry heading is the heading for the first named author.

More than Three Authors

Rule 21.6C2 states:

> If responsibility is shared among more than three persons or bodies and principal responsibility is not attributed to any ..., enter under title. Make an added entry under the heading for the first person or corporate body named.

So if a work has more than three personal authors, the main entry heading is the heading for the title.

Editorial Direction

Rule 21.7 states that if a work is produced under editorial direction, the main entry heading is the heading for the title.

Intellectual Responsibility?

However, sometimes an editor or compiler is responsible for the intellectual content of a work. A compiler of a glossary of terms, for example, has created the work by his or her own intellectual effort, and therefore heads the main entry.

Rules for Main Entry of Works of Personal Authorship

Rule 21.1A2 states:

> Enter a work by one or more persons under the heading for:
>> the personal author (21.4A)
>> the principal personal author (21.6B)
>> the probable personal author (21.5B).
>
> In some cases of
>> shared personal authorship (21.6) and
>> mixed personal authorship (21.8-21.27),
> enter under the heading for the person named first.

EXERCISE 10.1

Indicate the main entry for the following items, giving appropriate rule numbers to justify your answers. Do not try to format the headings correctly.

a.

> *The Larwood Story*
>
> •
>
> *HAROLD LARWOOD*
> *With*
> *KEVIN PERKINS*

Main entry:

b.

> **NATION**
> **THE LIFE OF AN INDEPENDENT**
> **JOURNAL OF OPINION**
> **1958-1972**
>
> edited and introduced by
> **K. S. INGLIS**
>
> assisted by
> Jan Brazier

Main entry:

c.

> # Maximising the Impact of Health Technology Assessment
>
> M. Drummond, D. Hailey, C. Selby Smith

Main entry:

d.

> ## INSTRUCTIONAL MEDIA AND TECHNOLOGIES FOR LEARNING
>
> ROBERT   HEINICH
> MICHAEL   MOLENDA
> JAMES D. RUSSELL
> SHARON E. SMALDINO

Main entry:

e.

> # LibrarySpeak
>
> ### A handbook of terms in librarianship and information management
>
> compiled by
> **Mary Mortimer**

Main entry:

f.

> ## THE
> ## NEW SHORTER
> ## OXFORD ENGLISH
> ## DICTIONARY
> ON HISTORICAL PRINCIPLES
>
> EDITED BY
> LESLEY BROWN

Main entry:

Modifications

AACR2 also has rules for works of mixed responsibility where works have been modified. Examples include a poem which has been translated, an adult novel which has been adapted for children, a piece of music differently arranged.

Rule 21.9A states:

> Enter a work that is a modification of another under the heading appropriate to the new work if the modification has substantially changed the nature and content of the original or if the medium of expression has been changed. If, however, the modification is an abridgement, rearrangement, etc., enter under the heading appropriate to the original ...

Adaptations for Children

Rule 21.10A states:

> Enter a paraphrase, ... adaptation for children ... under the heading for the adapter. If the adapter is unknown, enter under title.

Piccolo Adventure Library

The Last of the Mohicans

retold by Alan Robertshaw from the original by James Fenimore Cooper
text and cover illustrations by Tom Barling

Different Literary Form

Rule 21.10A again:

> Enter a paraphrase, ... or version in a different literary form (e.g., novelization, dramatization) under the heading for the adapter. If the adapter is unknown, enter under title.

Shakespeare's original works were plays. In any retelling of the plays in prose—that is, in a different literary form—the main entry will be under the heading for the person responsible for the new literary form.

CHARLES AND MARY LAMB

Tales from Shakespeare

Revisions

When a work has been revised, the main entry depends on whether or not the original author is still considered responsible for the work.

Rule 21.12A1 states:

> Enter ... under the heading for the original author if:
> a) the original author is named in a statement of responsibility in the item being cataloged ...

Cruden's Complete Concordance to the Old and New Testaments
with Notes and Biblical Proper Names under One Alphabetical Arrangement

BY ALEXANDER CRUDEN

REVISED AND EDITED BY
C. H. IRWIN, A. D. ADAMS, S. A. WATERS

Original Author No Longer Responsible

The original author is no longer considered to be responsible if, for example, the original author is named only in the title proper and some other person is named in the statement of responsibility or in the statement of responsibility relating to the edition (Rule 21.12B1).

CUNNINGHAM'S
MANUAL OF PRACTICAL ANATOMY

THIRTEENTH EDITION

REVISED BY
G. J. ROMANES

Illustrated Texts

The rules distinguish between a work in which an artist has provided illustrations for a text (Rule 21.11)

POEMS OF
HENRY LAWSON

Selected by Walter Stone   *Illustrated by Pro Hart*

and a work that is a collaboration between an artist and a writer (Rule 21.24).

MARS

*Arthur Boyd
and
Peter Porter*

(Arthur Boyd is a painter; Peter Porter is a poet)

Name-Title Added Entries

A name-title added entry heading consists of the name of a person or corporate body and the title of an item. It is made when the work being cataloged is related to another work, and we want users to find the author and title of the other work together as a heading,

e.g., Irving, Washington, 1783-1859. The Alhambra

EXERCISE 10.2

Indicate the main entry for the following items, giving appropriate rule numbers to justify your answers. Do not try to format the headings correctly.

a.

Robinson Crusoe

Daniel Defoe
Simplified by Michael West
Revised by D K Swan

1200 word
vocabulary

Main entry:

b.

> # MICHELANGELO
> PAINTINGS • SCULPTURES • ARCHITECTURE
> BY LUDWIG GOLDSCHEIDER

This book has a 4-page biography and a 14-page description of the works by Goldscheider, and 240 pages of reproductions of Michelangelo's works.

Main entry:

c.

> # petunia rose's gardening book
>
> **new edition**
> **revised by lily rose**

Main entry:

Works with a Collective Title

Rule 21.7B1 refers to works which are contributed to by different persons or bodies, and which have a collective title.

It states:

> Enter a work ... under its title if it has a collective title. Make added entries under the headings for the compilers/editors if there are not more than three and if they are named prominently in the item being cataloged.

> ## ALBINONI • HANDEL
> ## HERTEL • TELEMANN
>
> **Trumpet Concertos**

Works without a Collective Title

However there are also collections of works with no collective title.

Rule 21.7C1 states:

> If a work ... lacks a collective title, enter it under the heading appropriate to the first work ... named in the chief source of information ... Make added entries for editors/compilers and for the other works or contributors ...

BRAHMS
Symphony No. 2 in D major, Op. 73
SCHUBERT
Symphony No. 7 in B minor, D. 759

Corporate Body Main Entry

Enter a work under a corporate body main entry heading only in very explicit circumstances (detailed in Rule 21.1B2).

In brief, the main entry heading will be the corporate body if the work:
a) is of an administrative nature dealing with the corporate body itself
   or its internal policies, procedures, finances, and/or operations
   or its officers, staff, and/or membership (e.g., directories)
   or its resources (e.g., catalogs, inventories)

Handbook 1998

AMERICAN CONCRETE INSTITUTE
FARMINGTON HILLS, MICHIGAN

---

b) is a specified type of legal or religious work, such as a law, decree, constitution, treaty, court rules and decisions

---

NEBRASKA

PUBLIC TRANSPORTATION ACT 1984

---

c)   records the collective thought of the body as in the report of a commission, committee, etc., or official statement of position on external policies

```
        National Health and Medical Research Council
         Working Party on Management of Severe Pain


              Management of Severe Pain

                    Report of the
         Working Party on Management of Severe Pain
```

d)   reports the proceedings of a conference, expedition, event, etc.

```
        Council on Library/Media Technicians Inc.

        9th Biennial Conference and Exhibition

                    Proceedings
```

e)   results from the collective activity of a performing group where responsibility goes beyond just performance

f)   is a cartographic item emanating from a corporate body which does more than just publish, distribute, etc.

```
                  Royal Australian Survey Corps
            Australia 1:50 000 topographic survey: 2053 4


                  Cane River, Western Australia
            produced by the Royal Australian Survey Corps

                         Ed. 1-AAS
```

Consider main entry under a corporate body only if there is no personal author.

Rule 21.1B2 (c) assumes that the relevant members of the corporate body have all agreed to the content of the item. That is, the item expresses the **opinion** of the body, not just the opinions they have collected together from others.

In Rule 21.1B2 (d), note that the **conference itself** is the corporate body.

Rule 21.1B2 (e) applies to a performing group which is actually engaged in **creating** the work as it is performed. This is very unusual.

Rule 21.1B2 (f) is most often applied to maps in which a corporate body, for example a cartographic division of a larger body, has drawn and produced the map(s).

EXERCISE 10.3

Indicate the main entry for the following items, giving appropriate rule numbers to justify your answers. Do not try to format the headings correctly.

a. Fifty years of impressionism by Robert Moser
(This is the catalog of a loan exhibition held in the Museum of Art, Fairfield, Conn., June, 1998)

Main entry:

b. Membership directory of the American Bar Association

Main entry:

c. A room-by-room guide to the Cleveland Museum of Art by Melissa Cranshaw

Main entry:

d. Proceedings of the fifth annual Conference on Energy held in Philadelphia, January 5 to 7, 1997

Main entry:

e. Standards for air quality by the Standards Committee of the American Antipollution Society

Main entry:

f. Title page: National Campaign Against Drug Abuse. National Health Policy on Tobacco in Australia and Examples of strategies for implementation.

Foreword states: "The National Health Policy on Tobacco in Australia" was adopted by the Ministerial Council on Drug Strategy … The strategies contained in the document "Examples of strategies for implementation" are suggestions for ways in which the policy might be implemented.

Main entry:

    g.   The Anarchist Party Program in Ohio / by the Ohio Section of the Anarchist Party

                Main entry:

    h.   The annual report of the Trinidad Netball Association

                Main entry:

    i.   The National Association for the Advancement of Colored People's discussion paper "Police conduct in minority communities : an issue for your consideration"

                Main entry:

Title Main Entry

A record has a title main entry if:
- its author is unknown
- it has more than three authors
- it emanates from a corporate body, but does not fit into 21.1B2
- it is produced under editorial direction
- it is a sacred scripture.

Rule 21.1C lists these reasons.

Uniform Title

In the case of sacred scriptures, a special title known as a uniform title will sometimes be used. This is a special title added by the cataloger to:
(a) distinguish between works with identical titles;
(b) collocate identical works that have different titles;
(c) subarrange works of voluminous authors.

Uniform titles are treated in Chapter 16 of this book, Chapter 25 of *AACR2* and module 21 of CatSkill.

Does It Matter?

When catalog entries were written or typed one at a time, the main entry contained all the necessary information. Added entries could then be shortened, to save work. When catalog entries are all reproduced mechanically, each entry contains the same information, except for the heading.

Automated catalogs allow users to find records from a large number of access points. In many catalogs, it no longer matters which is the main and which are the added entries.

Sometimes It Matters

When a manual catalog has only one full entry, which is found by the use of indexes, it is useful to know which it is likely to be.

For example, many bibliographies, including national bibliographies, have one main classified sequence with complete catalog entries. Access to these complete entries is by looking up an author index, a title index or a subject index.

Added Entries

Added entries are made to enable users to find an item, and to bring related materials together in the catalog.

Added entries can be
- names of persons
- names of corporate bodies
- titles
- series
- name/title access points (for related works).

Chapter 21 tells us which added entries to make. Chapters 22-25 tells us how to set up the particular form of the headings.

Rules for Added Entries

Rule 21.29 encourages us to make as many added entries as are necessary to provide access to the records in the catalog, "in the context of a given catalog".

Rule 21.30 give specific rules for added entries:
- 2 or more persons or bodies involved (21.30A)
- collaborators (21.30B)
- writers (21.30C)
- editors and compilers (21.30D)
- corporate bodies (21.30E)
- other related persons or bodies (21.30F)
- related works (21.30G)
- other relationships (21.30H)
- titles (21.30J)
- translators (21.30K1)
- illustrators (21.30K2)
- series (21.30L)
- analytical entries (21.30M).

You will need to consult the specific rules, particularly for the special cases:
- translators (21.30K1)
- illustrators (21.30K2)
- series (21.30L)
- analytical entries (21.30M).

Changes in Title Proper (21.2)

Sometimes very similar works are published and it becomes necessary to inspect the title very closely in order to identify the differences. The rules aim to keep cataloging of new materials to a minimum, so similar material can be treated as copies rather than new items.

Check Rule 21.2A if you think you are cataloging a work with a change of title proper.

If you do not consider the title to have changed, give details in a note, and make an added entry for any variant titles needed for access.

When a monograph appears in a different edition, regardless of title, a new record is always created.

EXERCISE 10.4

Indicate main entry and added entries for the following titles, giving appropriate rule numbers to justify your answers. The examples may refer to any of the rules in Chapter 21. Do not try to format the headings correctly.

a. Title page: World climate, by John S. Herrold and Ruth Fairchild-Carruthers. (Originally published as Our changing climate)

   Main entry:

   Added entries:

b. Title page: A bibliography on weather, compiled by Roberta Jackson Hunt

   Main entry:

   Added entries:

c. Title page: The message of President Theodore Roosevelt to the Congress, September 8, 1904

   Main entry:

   Added entries:

d.   Title page: A country adventure: a play, by Enid McFall. (A rewriting of the novel, Weir of Hermiston, by Robert Louis Stevenson)

       Main entry:

       Added entries:

e.   Title page: The complete poetry of Marianne Moore, with an introduction by Simon Suggs

       Main entry:

       Added entries:

f.   The birds, by Aristophanes, translated into English by Robert Minton Blake. (This is the most recent of many translations)

       Main entry:

       Added entries:

g.   The autobiography of Frodo (a character, Hobbit of the Shire, in The lord of the rings, by J. R. R. Tolkien) as reported to Chela Ormond

       Main entry:

       Added entries:

h.   Crafts of the past, by Louis Brogan, Henrietta LaMont, Joseph Ricardo and Florence W. Eames

       Main entry:

       Added entries:

i.   Readings in ethics, compiled by Louise Allenby and Kelly Bryant. Second revised edition revised by R. K. Smith

       Main entry:

       Added entries:

j.   Three plays by contemporary American women /edited and with an introduction by Honor Moore. (Contents: The abdication / Wolff, R. – The ice wolf / Kraus, J. – I lost a pair of gloves yesterday / Lamb, M.)

EXERCISE 10.5

Indicate main entry and added entries for the following titles, giving appropriate rule numbers to justify your answers. The examples may refer to any of the rules in Chapter 21. Do not try to format the headings correctly.

a.

> Introducing WordPerfect 5.1 / Elizabeth Bromham. – 3rd ed. –
> Palo Alto, Calif. : Daybreak Publishing, 1992. – vi, 98 p. : ill. ; 21
> cm. – (Daybreak computer series)
> Previous ed.: 1990.
> Includes index.
> ISBN 1-875584-00-5 : $14.95

Main entry:

Added entries:

b.

> Computerized financial and management accounting / S.
> Roberts, R. Cuthbert, L. Comley. – Albany, N.Y. : Coriolanis
> Books, c1998. – viii, 241 p. : ill. ; 25 cm. + 1 computer disk (5
> 1/4 in.). – (Focus on accounting series)
> For senior college students.
> ISBN 0-7306-0173-0

Main entry:

Added entries:

c.

> How to hold an audience without a rope / Clifford Warne and
> Paul White. – [Rev. ed.] – Little Rock, Ark. : Scripture Union,
> 1996, c1982. – x, 83 p. ; 18 cm.
> ISBN 0-85892-512-5

Main entry:

Added entries:

d.

Learning to care for our environment : Maine's environmental education strategy. – Portland, Me. : Maine Environmental Education Council, 1995. – 41 p., [2] leaves of plates : ill. (some col.) ; 30 cm.
ISBN 0-73063-094-3

(This is a set of ideas about how to implement the strategy. It is not the official position of the Council.)

Main entry:

Added entries:

e.

Secondary employment of Jacksonville police officers : corruption prevention project, August 1984 / Independent Commission Against Corruption. – Jacksonville, Fla. : The Commission, 1992. – vi, 65, [38] p. ; 30 cm.
Includes bibliography.
ISBN 0730599590

(This is an official ICAC report on this project.)

Main entry:

Added entries:

f.

What Black politicians are saying / edited by Nathan Wright, Jr.; introduction by Julian Bond. - New York : Hawthorn Books, [1972]. - xxvii, 210 p. ; 22 cm.

Main entry:

Added entries:

g.

> The Cambridge history of Pacific Islanders / edited by Donald
> Denoon ... [et al.]. – Cambridge : Cambridge University Press,
> 1997. – xvi, 518 p. : maps ; 24 cm.
> Bibliography: p.471-493.
> Includes index.
> ISBN 0-521-44195-1

Main entry:

Added entries:

h.

> The joy of ragtime [music] : a graded collection of classic piano
> rags by Scott Joplin, James Scott, Joseph F. Lamb, Tom Turpin,
> Charles Hunter, Percy Wenrich and many others / selected and
> edited by Denes Agay. – New York : Yorktown Music Press,
> c1974. – 80 p. ; 31 cm. – (The joy books)

Main entry:

Added entries:

Chapter 11
AUTHORITY CONTROL AND REFERENCES
(CatSkill—modules 16 & 22)

Authority Control
Authority control is the maintenance of standard forms of headings in the catalog, so that library users can locate information using consistent subject, name and title headings.

Some libraries record the standard forms of headings in an authority file, so that catalogers can refer to them, and not have to re-create them or look them up again. References made to and from the headings are also recorded here. Other libraries rely on the standardized headings available in their automated system. In either case, it is important to appreciate the need for standardized headings and the procedures required to establish and make use of them.

There are four types of authority records: Name, Subject, Series, and Uniform title. Name authority files generally include uniform titles.

Establishing the authority records involves the use of *AACR2* rules to decide on the correct form of the heading. It may also require reference sources to find dates of birth or full names.

Authority Files
There are several large authority files to which catalogers refer. The organizations which create them use *AACR2* rules and have access to additional information needed to establish the heading.

The largest authority file for descriptive cataloging is *Library of Congress name authorities*. It is issued quarterly on microfiche and cumulates at the end of every year. The headings are also contained in a number of commercially available products and systems.

If a library maintains its own authority file, it establishes authoritative headings using *Library of Congress name authorities* and other specialist authority files. It may add extra references, depending on the needs of its users.

References
A reference is a direction or signpost in the catalog from one heading to another, so that clients can find all related entries.

When we have a standard heading, we refer users to this heading from other headings which they may look up. Many library systems do this automatically, and users may be unaware that the terms they enter are not the preferred terms. Other systems show the correct headings, but users must select them to find the items they want. Where necessary, directions are provided in the catalog, pointing from unused headings to the headings which are used. Directions are also given to and from related items to link them together.

In all systems, the cataloger decides on the preferred heading(s), and enters the information into the system. This chapter treats references as if the cataloger needs to create them.

Chapter 26

Comprehensive rules for references are contained in Chapter 26 of *AACR2*.

In general, we make a reference under any heading a catalog user may reasonably expect to find. We must ensure that for every reference, there is an item in the catalog under the heading being used. That is, we must not direct catalog users to an empty space.

Libraries have traditionally needed to keep a record of all references made, so that they can be corrected or deleted. A library's own authority file fulfils this purpose. Increasingly, this control is incorporated into the operation of automated library systems.

Authority Records

The availability of authority records, and their precise format, is changing with developments in library systems. However, the principles of establishing standard forms of headings and enabling catalog users to find what they are looking for remain unchanged.

You will need to familiarize yourself with the authority records your library system uses. The examples are provided to show the structure of authority records, rather than any specific authority file.

LIBRARY OF CONGRESS NAME AUTHORITIES ONLINE (NOVEMBER 1998)

Here are the results of searching for the preferred heading for J. K. Galbraith:
>
> Heading: Galbraith, John Kenneth, 1908-
> References: Galbraith, J. K. (John Kenneth), 1908-
>   Gçelbreæit, Dzhon Kennet, 1908-
>   Gçelbreæit, Dzh. K. (Dzhon Kennet), 1908-

So, Galbraith, John Kenneth, 1908- is the heading we need.

LIBRARY OF CONGRESS NAME AUTHORITIES (CUMULATIVE MICROFICHE EDITION 1987-1995)

Library of Congress name authorities provides the preferred headings for a very large number of names. Since many names are identical, records also provide one or more sources of information by which searchers can identify the person they want. In this record for Mary Robinson, former president of Ireland, two sources of information are given. The first is a biography by F. Finlay, which establishes that this is the former Irish president. The second is a reference work used to verify her date of birth.

Robinson, Mary, 1944-
> Found:
>> Finlay, F. Mary Robinson, 1990: p.7 (Nov. 9, 1990,
>>> declared elected president of Ireland)
>> Who's who, what's what & where in Ireland, 1973
>>> (Robinson, Mary T.W., senator; b. Ballina, Co. Mayo.
>>> 5-21-1944; maiden name Bourke; m. 12-70 Nicholas
>>> Robinson)

EXERCISE 11.1

In LCNA or another online authority file, enter your own name or the name of an author. Make sure you can identify the preferred heading, and see if there are any other forms of the name which refer you to the preferred form.

Name:

Preferred form of heading:

Other (non-preferred) forms of name:

See Reference

A *see* reference directs the user from the form of a heading which is **not used** to a form of heading that is used.

Non-Preferred Form

When we have decided on one form of a name to be used as the standard heading, we need to refer the user **to** this heading **from** all the other headings they might reasonably look up.

Although Malcolm X's books are all published under this later name, users may look up his earlier name, Malcolm Little. So we make a *see* reference which will direct them to our preferred heading:

> Little, Malcolm
> see
> X, Malcolm

Change of Name

The folksinger and songwriter changed his name from Bob Camp to Hamilton Camp.

Our heading will therefore be: Camp, Hamilton

If the library changes all its headings to Camp, Hamilton, the reference will be:
> Camp, Bob
> see
> Camp, Hamilton

If the library has too many records with the heading Camp, Bob, they may choose to change to the new heading for new items, but for the older records make a reference:
> Camp, Bob
> see also
> Camp, Hamilton

In this case, they would also need the reference:
> Camp, Hamilton
> see also
> Camp, Bob

Different Entry Element

The preferred heading for Simone de Beauvoir is Beauvoir, Simone de, 1908-1986. However, catalog users might reasonably look up De Beauvoir, Simone.

The reference will look like this:
> De Beauvoir, Simone, 1908-1986
> see
> Beauvoir, Simone de, 1908-1986

See Also Reference

A *see also* reference directs the catalog user to a related entry or name. It is normally used when a person or corporate body is entered under two or more different names.

More than One Name

Many writers use more than one name for different types of writing. The academic Carolyn Heilbrun writes detective fiction under the pseudonym Amanda Cross. To link these names in the catalog, we use *see also* references. For example,
> Heilbrun, Carolyn
> see also
> Cross, Amanda

and

> Cross, Amanda
> see also
> Heilbrun, Carolyn

Change of Name of Corporate Body

Corporate bodies frequently change their names. In an authority file all the names are recorded, together with relevant information about how they are used and when changes have occurred.

When a corporate body changes its name, we link the names with *see also* references.

Here are the *see also* references for one name change. If the body changes its name more than once, references are also made, provided that there is a record which uses each of the names. Remember not to send users to headings if there is no record when they get there!

Association of Young People's Librarians (U.S.)
    see also the later heading
    American Library Association. Young Adult Services Division

    and

American Library Association. Young Adult Services Division
    see also the earlier heading
    Association of Young People's Librarians (U.S.)

In this example, the authority record (used by catalogers) notes the references to and from the heading.

AUTHORITY RECORD
Cleveland Home for Aged Colored People (Cleveland, Ohio)
    search also under the later heading
    Eliza Bryant Home for the Aged (Cleveland, Ohio)

Cleveland Home for Aged Colored People (Cleveland, Ohio)
    x x   Eliza Bryant Home for the Aged (Cleveland, Ohio) [later heading]

This generates the following references in the catalog:

REFERENCES IN THE CATALOG
Cleveland Home for Aged Colored People (Cleveland, Ohio)
    search also under the later heading
    Eliza Bryant Home for the Aged (Cleveland, Ohio)

Eliza Bryant Home for the Aged (Cleveland, Ohio)
    search also under the earlier heading
    Cleveland Home for Aged Colored People (Cleveland, Ohio)

Explanatory Reference

An explanatory reference provides more detailed guidance than is given in a *see* or *see also* reference. For example:

    Zambia. President (1964-1991 : Kaunda)
        Here are entered works by the President acting in his official
        capacity. For works by the President acting as an individual
            see also
        Kaunda, Kenneth D. (Kenneth David), 1924-

Many explanatory references are found in major authority files. Others are created by individual libraries to explain particular cataloging usage and practices.

Preferred Heading

A preferred heading is recorded together with the non-preferred headings for which references have been made. The non-preferred headings are marked with x or UF.

For example,

> IFLA Office for International Lending
>   x   International Federation of Library Associations.
>   Office for International Lending

or

> IFLA Office for International Lending
>   UF   International Federation of Library Associations.
>   Office for International Lending

That is, use the heading
IFLA Office for International Lending

and make a *see* reference from:
International Federation of Library Associations. Office for International Lending.

We also record the reference

> International Federation of Library Associations. Office for International Lending
>   See   IFLA Office for International Lending

EXERCISE 11.2

1.   *Library of Congress name authorities* lists the following:

> NABAC, the Association for Bank Audit, Control and Operation. Research Institute
>   x NABAC Research Institute

a.   Which is the preferred heading?

b.   Should they both be used?

c.   Make the appropriate reference for the catalog.

2. From this record, make the appropriate catalog references, assuming your library has works published under both names.

> National Food Processors Association (U.S.)
> > search also under the former name
> National Canners Association

A More Complicated Example

Sometimes the entry is quite complicated. For example, Bill Clinton could be entered under
*   Clinton, Bill (by which he is best known)
*   Clinton, William Jefferson (his full name) or
*   Blythe, William Jefferson (his birth name).

He has been
*   an individual
*   governor of Arkansas
*   president of the United States.

Here is part of the LCNA entry:

```
Clinton, Bill, 1946-
    Found
            WWA 1980/81 (Clinton, William J., b. 8-19-46; governor
                of Ark., 1979-    )
            Washington Post, 21 Jan. 1993: (William Jefferson Clinton elected 42nd
                President of the United States)
            Washington Post, Book world, Aug. 16, 1992: p.9 (Gov. Bill Clinton of Arkansas;
                son of William Blythe; father killed in a car accident 3 months before Bill
                was born; William Jefferson Blythe IV, b. 8/19/1946;  later adopted the
                name of his first stepfather, Roger Clinton)
    x   Clinton, William J. (William Jefferson), 1946-
    x   Blythe, William Jefferson, 1946-
    xx  Arkansas. Governor (1979-1981 : Clinton)
    xx  Arkansas. Governor (1983-1992 : Clinton)
    xx  United States. President (1993- : Clinton)
```

" x   Clinton, William J. (William Jefferson), 1946-" means to make a *see* reference from this heading to the preferred heading, which is given at the top of the entry.

It will result in the entry:
Clinton, William J. (William Jefferson), 1946-
          search under
    Clinton, Bill, 1946-

"x x   Arkansas. Governor (1979-1981   : Clinton)" means to make a *see also* reference from this heading to the main heading.

It will result in the entry:
Arkansas. Governor (1979-1981 : Clinton)
          search also under
    Clinton, Bill, 1946-

EXERCISE 11.3

Make the catalog references which result from the following authority records. If you have difficulty, look up each form of the name in *Library of Congress name authorities*, and study the references given.

a.   Clinton, Bill, 1946-
             x   Blythe, William Jefferson, 1946-

b.   Clinton, Bill, 1946-
             xx   Arkansas. Governor (1983-1992 : Clinton)

c.   Clinton, Bill, 1946-
             xx   United States. President (1993- : Clinton)

Series Authority Files

A series authority file records every series represented in the catalog, and may indicate whether an added entry is made for the series (i.e., whether the series is traced). It may also indicate whether any references are required and if works in a series are classified together (at a common call number) or classified separately.

An entry should be made for every new series recording the decisions made.

AUTHORITY FILE

        Foreign agriculture economic report

    x   United States. Dept. of Agriculture. Foreign agriculture economic report

        Traced (or used for series added entry)

        Classified at HD1411.F59

CATALOG ENTRY

        United States. Dept. of Agriculture. Foreign agriculture economic report
          See (or USE)
              Foreign agriculture economic report

Chapter 12
HEADINGS FOR PERSONS
(CatSkill—module 17)

Introduction
AACR2 provides rules to establish headings for persons in the catalog, so that library users can locate these names using consistent headings. When users search for a particular person, they need to be able to find all other works by this person under the same form of his or her name.

If authors have published other works under different forms of their name, the catalog can link the works together by using the same heading and references from other forms of the name.

Chapter 22
The rules for headings for persons are contained in Chapter 22 of *AACR2*. A brief summary of the most important rules is included here. You will need to consult the rules themselves for details and examples.

First, we must decide on the name to be used.

Second, we need to establish the entry element—that is, the part of the name under which the name will be found in the catalog.

Choice of Name (22.1)
Choose the name most frequently used by the person. It may be:
- real name
- pseudonym
- title of nobility
- nickname
- initials
- including accents and hyphens
or something else.

It is usually the name which appears on the chief source of information (title page, etc.) of works by the person.

Predominant Name (22.2A)
If a person is known by more than one name, choose the name by which the person is clearly more commonly known.

Check the authority file to verify the heading.

Galbraith, John Kenneth *not* Galbraith, J. K. *or* Galbraith, (J. K.) John Kenneth

Separate Identities (22.2B2)

Sometimes the same person has written different kinds of works under different names. Each name is used with the work it relates to.

Cross, Amanda, 1926-. The puzzled heart (detective fiction)   *These are the*
Heilbrun, Carolyn G., 1926-. The education of a woman (biography)   *same person*

Change of Name (22.2C)

Choose the latest form of name unless there is reason to believe the earlier name will persist.

Muhammad Ali *not* Cassius Clay

Entry Element (22.4)

This is the part of the name under which the name will be found in the catalog.

Bronte, Charlotte *not* Charlotte Bronte

Use the Surname (22.5)

Use the surname if there is one.

If the first element is a surname, follow it by a comma. If the surname is not first, turn the name around so that the surname is the first element. Follow it by a comma.

Mao, Tse-tung
Walker, Alice

Compound Surnames (22.5C)

A compound surname consists of two or more proper names, sometimes connected by a hyphen, a conjunction and/or a preposition.

David Lloyd George
Henrietta Drake-Brockman
Vincent van Gogh
Daphne du Maurier
Georg Ludwig von und zu Urff

In general, use the element preferred by the person bearing the name. If this is not known, use the element preferred in reference sources in the person's language or country of residence.

Lloyd George, David

If the surname is hyphenated, enter under the first element.

Drake-Brockman, Henrietta

If it is not hyphenated, check Rules 22.5C4-22.5C5. If you are not sure that it is a compound surname, check Rule 22.5C6.

If the name has one or more separately written prefixes—e.g., articles and prepositions or a combination of the two—check the language groupings in Rule 22.5D1, since the practice is different in different languages.

> Musset, Alfred de (French)
> Du Maurier, Daphne (English)

Other Forms
Chapter 22 gives rules for the headings of many other kinds of names. They include:
> Entry under title of nobility
> Entry under given name
> Entry under initials, letters, or numerals
> Entry under phrase.

Additions to Names
Chapter 22 contains detailed rules about additions to names, for example:
> Titles of nobility
> British terms of honor
> Saints
> Spirits
> Additions to surname only
> Royalty
> Popes
> Bishops
> Other persons of religious vocation.

Distinguishing Identical Names
There are several rules for distinguishing names which are or might be identical. They include the addition of a person's full name and dates of birth and death. This is the practice followed by the major cataloging agencies and networks.

When a library catalog uses the headings established in one of the major name authority files, it makes use of this provision in the rules.

Dates (22.17)
The dates normally used are the date of birth and, where the person is no longer living, the date of death.

> Browne, John, 1642-ca. 1700
> Browne, John, 1696-1750

It is an option to add date(s) to all personal names, even if it is not necessary to distinguish between headings.

> Shakespeare, William, 1554-1616

If these dates cannot be established, Rule 22.17A gives examples of other dates which can be used.

> Browne, John, b. 1668 or 9
> Browne, John, fl. 1777-1798

Fuller Forms (22.18)

If a fuller form of a person's name is known, and the person does not commonly use the fuller form, add the fuller form to distinguish between headings that are otherwise identical.

> Johnston, J. A. (John Anthony)
> Johnston, J. A. (Judith A.)

Distinguishing Terms (22.19)

Rule 22.19 lists some other terms which can be used to distinguish between identical headings.

> Johnson, Fred, 1916-
> Johnson, Fred, vocalist

Certain Languages

Rules 22.21 through 22.28 treat in more detail names not written in the roman alphabet and names in non-European languages written in the roman alphabet.

It would be wise to consult a name authority file if you need to establish any of these name headings.

When in Doubt ...

Standard forms of name for headings are best established by using a large authority file. You are strongly advised always to check the forms of names used as headings in an authority file such as *Library of Congress name authorities.*

In Summary

- Choose the most commonly used name (real, pseudonym, initials, etc.).
- Decide which part of the name comes first in the heading (entry element).
- Make the name distinct if necessary.

EXERCISE 12.1

Using *AACR2*, give the correct form of the following personal names. Rule numbers have been given for some examples.

a. Francis Scott Fitzgerald (known as Francis Scott Fitzgerald in his works), born 1896 and died 1940 - Rule 22.18

b. Leong Ka Tai (Leong is the surname) - Rule 22.4B2

c. Samuel Raymond Brown (born in 1918 and still alive; sometimes uses S. R. Brown, although Samuel Raymond Brown is the most common name in his works) - Rules 22.18, 22.17

d. José María Escrivá de Balaguer (Escrivá de Balaguer is a Spanish compound surname); born 1902, died 1975 - Rule 22.5D1

e. Claudio Vita-Finzi - Rule 22.5C3

f. Josephine Blanche D'Alpuget, born 1944, never uses her first name - Rule 22.1A

g. Maurice Pascal Alers Hankey, the Baron Hankey, 1877-1963 - Rule 22.6A

h. Philip the Second the King of Spain, born 1527, died 1598 - Rule 22.16A

i. Henry Handel Richardson (whose real name was Henrietta) - Rule 22.5C6

j. Carson McCullers, lived 1917 to 1967

k. Norman Mailer

l. Tomie de Paola is an American writer of Italian descent

EXERCISE 12.2

Using an authority file, give the correct form of the following personal names. Indicate any references needed.

a.   Samuel Langhorne Clemens wrote under the pseudonym Mark Twain; he lived from 1835 to 1910

b.   Pedro Henríquez Ureña, born 1884, died 1946

c.   Marjorie Kinnan Baskin, 1896-1953, who became Marjorie Kinnan Rawlings and wrote all her work under this name

d.   Angelo Giuseppi Roncalli became Pope John XXIII; the official Latin form of the name is Joannes

e.   Margaret Atwood, born 1939, who prefers her full name Margaret Eleanor Atwood

f.   Cicely Isabel Fairfield married and became Cecily Andrews; she changed her name to Rebecca West and used this name for all her writing

g.   George Bernard Shaw is also known as G. B. Shaw and Bernard Shaw

h. The author's name appears in various places as Nicholas Kazan, Nikos Kasantzakis and Nikosz Kasandzakisz; in English translations of his works his surname usually appears as Nikos Kazantzakis

i. Edgar Allan Poe, 1809-1849

j. Robert Penn Warren, born 1905-, who sometimes referred to himself as Red

MARC

Names are coded in the same way as the description, by referring to the MARC codes at the back of the book (or the MARC manual if you have access to it). First you need to know whether the name is a main or an added entry, and then use the tag, indicators and subfield codes you need.

EXERCISE 12.3

Here are some of the names from Exercise 12.1. Code them as main entries.

a. Fitzgerald, F. Scott (Francis Scott), 1896-1940

    100

b. Leong, Ka Tai

    100

c. Brown, Samuel Raymond, 1918-

    100

d. Escrivá de Balaguer, José María, 1902-1975

    100

e.   Vita-Finzi, Claudio

100

EXERCISE 12.4
Here are more of the names from Exercise 12.1. Code them as added entries.

a.   D'Alpuget, Blanche, 1944-

700

b.   McCullers, Carson, 1917-1967

700

c.   Philip II, King of Spain, 1527-1598

700

d.   Richardson, Henry Handel

700

e.   Hankey, Maurice Pascal Alers Hankey, Baron, 1877-1963

700

Title Added Entry
A normal title added entry does not need additional coding, since it is already included in the description. The first indicator in the title field tells the computer whether or not to make a title added entry.

Variant Title Added Entry
A variant title is a title other than the title proper, by which the work is also known.

Adobe Photoshop *is also known as* Photoshop

When a work needs an additional access point for the variant title, it will be coded using the 246 (Varying Form of Title) field.

Name-Title Added Entry

A name-title added entry is an added entry consisting of the name of a person or corporate body and the title of an item.

When a MARC record includes a name-title added entry, it is coded using one of the fields
    700 (Added Entry—Personal Name)
    710 (Added Entry—Corporate Name)

The title is coded in a subfield of this field. Automated systems pick up the title from this subfield and create another title access point.

EXERCISE 12.5

Go back to the descriptions in Chapters 7-9 which have only personal name (and title and series) main and added entries, decide on the entries, and format and code them. Answers are given at the back of the book.

Chapter 13
GEOGRAPHIC NAMES AS HEADINGS
(CatSkill—module 18)

Introduction
AACR2 provides rules for establishing standard geographic names in the catalog, so that library users can locate places and bodies using consistent headings.

Many places have more than one form of name. A catalog needs a standard form of geographic name for each place.

Chapter 23
The rules for geographic names are contained in Chapter 23 of *AACR2*.

Geographic names are used:
• to distinguish between corporate bodies with the same name
• as additions to other corporate names
• as the names of governments and communities that are not governments.

General Rule (23.2)
The general rule is to use the English form if it is commonly used. Reference sources may be needed to decide the common English form. Where there is no English name in general use, use the official name of the place. If there is more than one official name, the English name is preferred.

As with other names, it is always best to verify a geographic name in a name authority file. The Library of Congress has preferences for certain names, e.g., Great Britain (*not* United Kingdom), United States (*not* United States of America).

Changes of Name (23.3)
If the name of a place changes, we use each name to refer to the place at the time a particular name was used.

Additions to Names (23.4)
In general, the rules aim to:
• identify a place by using the name of a larger place
• distinguish between two or more places with the same name.

Chapter 23 details the additions for particular regions, including Australia, Canada, Malaysia, the United States, the U.S.S.R., Yugoslavia, and the British Isles. Although the U.S.S.R. and Yugoslavia are no longer political entities, the rules apply to earlier publications of those places. They also apply to current publications of the individual countries (previously republics).

No Addition Needed

The names of countries do not require any qualification. Nor do the parts of the British Isles: England, the Republic of Ireland, Northern Ireland, Scotland, Wales, the Isle of Man, the Channel Islands. States, provinces, territories, etc., of Australia, Canada, Malaysia, the United States, the U.S.S.R., and Yugoslavia also stand on their own.

E.g., Scotland
      Kansas

Addition Needed

Places within some states, territories and parts of the British Isles require qualification by the name of the larger area. Refer to Rules 23.4C through 23F.

If the place is in a state, province, territory, etc., of Australia, Canada, Malaysia, the United States, the U.S.S.R., or Yugoslavia, add the name of the state, etc., in which it is located.

E.g., Kansas City (Kan.)
      Victoria (B.C.)

If the place is in England, the Republic of Ireland, Northern Ireland, Scotland, Wales, the Isle of Man, or the Channel Islands, add England, Ireland, Northern Ireland, Scotland, Wales, Isle of Man, or Channel Islands.

E.g., Strathclyde (Scotland)
      Jersey (Channel Islands)

EXERCISE 13.1

Establish the correct *AACR2* form of the following places. Verify in *Library of Congress name authorities* if possible:

a.   Washington, D.C.

b.   Washington State

c.   Mt. Pleasant (Texas)

d.   Vancouver Island

e.   Antarctic regions

f.   Addis Ababa

g.   New York City

h.   New York State

i.   Acadia N. P.

j.   Montreal in Quebec

k.   Ayrshire, a county in Scotland

l.   East Pakistan which is now Bangladesh—make both headings and the references between them. (Only do this in a library if you have items both before and after the founding of the new nation.)

Chapter 14
HEADINGS FOR CORPORATE BODIES
(CatSkill—module 19)

Introduction
AACR2 provides rules for establishing headings for corporate bodies in the catalog, so that users can locate these names using consistent headings. It is important to establish standard forms of name for corporate bodies, so that there is a consistent access point for each body.

References can be made from other forms of the name.

Chapter 24
The rules for headings for corporate bodies are contained in Chapter 24 of *AACR2*. A brief summary of the most important rules is included here. You will need to consult the rules themselves for details and examples.

Direct Name (24.1A)
Choose the name by which the corporate body is commonly identified.

Enter the body directly under its own name if:
• the body is known under that name
• it does not need the name of another body or government to identify it.

> Center for Technology Transfer & Pollution Prevention

Change of Name (24.1C)
Corporate bodies often change their names.

Make a new heading under the new name for items appearing under that name. Use the form in use at the time of publication of the work. Make references from the old heading to the new and from the new heading to the old, provided you have works under both headings.

Variant Names (24.2)
Sometimes corporate bodies use more than one form of their name.

Choose the form of name in the chief sources of information. If this varies, choose the name that is presented formally. If no name is presented formally, or if all names are presented formally, use the predominant form of name.

If there is no predominant form, use a brief form (including an initialism or acronym) that would differentiate the body from others with the same or similar brief names. Special rules for variant names are given in Rule 24.3.

Conventional Name (24.3C)

Use the conventional name.

> Westminster Abbey *not* Collegiate Church of St. Peter in Westminster

Governments (24.3E)

Use the conventional name of a government, unless the official name is in common use. The conventional name of a government is the geographic name of the area over which the government exercises jurisdiction.

> Puerto Rico *not* Commonwealth of Puerto Rico

Additions to the Name (24.4)

In general, we make additions to the names of corporate bodies
- to convey the idea of a corporate body, or
- to distinguish between similar names, or
- to assist in understanding the nature or purpose of the body.

> Mayflower (Ship)
> Mayflower (Ship : Replica)

Omissions (24.5)

In general, omit initial articles and adjectival terms or abbreviations indicating incorporation.

> Library Association *not* The Library Association
> Events Unlimited *not* Events Unlimited Inc.

Governments. Additions (24.6)

Add terms to the names of governments which are otherwise the same.

> Guadalajara (Mexico)
> Guadalajara (Spain)
>
> New York (N.Y.)
> New York (State)

EXERCISE 14.1

Write these names in the correct *AACR2* form. After you have decided, check them in *LCNA*.

a.   ICI Limited

b.   Music Educators National Conference

c.   Duke University of Durham, North Carolina

d.   Missouri Clean Water Commission

e.   The Lao People's Democratic Republic

f.   United Nations International Children's Emergency Fund (UNICEF)

g.   Native Plant Society of Oregon

h.   The Reference Book Division of the National Underwriter Company

i.   The New York Times newspaper

j.   The Australian newspaper

Subordinate Bodies (24.12)

If the name of a corporate body is distinctive, it is entered directly under its own name. However, there are some types of corporate bodies which can only be identified as part of a larger body.

For example, a department or a branch is always part of a parent body, and can only be identified by including the name of the parent body.

> University of Pittsburgh. Research Bureau for Retail Training
> Canadian Broadcasting Corporation. Service de linguistique et de traduction

Types of Subordinate Body (24.13)

Rule 24.13 lists six types of subordinate body to be entered under the name of the parent body. They include names which imply administrative subordination, are general in nature, do not convey the idea of a corporate body or include the entire name of the higher or related body.

> Daughters of the American Revolution. Columbus Chapter

Subheadings

Sometimes a corporate body is part of a larger body which is itself part of a still larger body.

For example, the Audiovisual Committee is part of the Public Library Association, which is part of the American Library Association. However, the Public Library Association can be entered under its own name.

So the heading is:
> Public Library Association. Audiovisual Committee

Omit Part of Hierarchy

It is sometimes necessary only to include some of the corporate bodies in the hierarchy.

Here is a hierarchy:
> American Dietetic Association
> House of Delegates
> Committee on Association Membership

We need a heading for the Committee.

Could we leave out the Committee on Association Membership? No, since this is the body for which we are making the heading.

Could we leave out the House of Delegates? Yes, since the Committee on Association Membership is the only committee of this name in the American Dietetic Association, and therefore we do not need the House of Delegates to identify it.

So our heading will be:
> American Dietetic Association. Committee on Association Membership

References

When we omit part of a hierarchy, we need to make references from fuller headings which users might expect to find.

Here is our original hierarchy:
> American Dietetic Association
> House of Delegates
> Committee on Association Membership

And here is the hierarchy we have decided on:
> American Dietetic Association
> Committee on Association Membership

We make a *see* reference from
> American Dietetic Association
> House of Delegates
> Committee on Association Membership

> to
> American Dietetic Association
> Committee on Association Membership

which looks like this:
> American Dietetic Association. House of Delegates. Committee on Association
> Membership
> > see
> > > American Dietetic Association. Committee on Association Membership

Government Bodies (24.17)

The same general principle applies to government bodies. If a body has a name which is distinctive and identifiable, enter it under its own name.

> Appalachian Education Satellite Program

Rule 24.17 gives a list of types of bodies which must include the name of the government which creates or controls them. They include names which imply administrative subordination, are general in nature, do not convey the idea of a corporate body and do not include the name of the government.

They also include official arms of government:
- a ministry
- a legislative body
- a court
- a principal service of the armed forces
- a head of state or head of government
- an embassy, consulate, etc.
- a delegation to an international or intergovernmental body.

Subheadings

Again, we apply the same principle as for non-government bodies. In a hierarchy of subordinate bodies, leave out any that are not needed for identification of the body.

Here is a hierarchy:
> United States
> Dept. of Education
> Office of Elementary and Secondary Education

We need a heading for the Office of Elementary and Secondary Education.

We must retain the heading United States, since that is the name of the government. Is this (likely to be) the only Office of Elementary and Secondary Education in the government of the United States?

Yes, it is, so we can omit Dept. of Education from the hierarchy, and still retain all the elements we need to identify our government body.

Our heading is now:
> United States. Office of Elementary and Secondary Education

Special Rules

Chapter 24 also contains rules for:
- government officials
- legislative bodies
- constitutional conventions
- courts
- armed forces
- embassies, consulates, etc.
- delegations to international and intergovernmental bodies
- religious bodies and officials.

References

When corporate bodies change their names, references must be made to and from the different forms of the names. References must also be made to and from variant forms of the name of a body.

When one or more body is omitted from a hierarchy of subordinate bodies, references must be made from the fuller form of the heading.

Name Authority File

As with other names, the correct form of name for a corporate body should always be checked in a name authority file.

In Summary

Feature of Corporate Body	Rule Number
Change of name	24.1C
Variant names for the same body	24.2, 24.3
Initials and/or acronyms used as the predominant form	24.1, 24.2D
Name is not clearly a corporate body	24.4B
Same names for different bodies	24.4C
Corporate name includes unnecessary words	24.5
Same names for government bodies	24.6
Same names for different conferences	24.7
Sections of a corporate/government body	24.12, 24.13, 24.14, 24.17, 24.18, 24.19

EXERCISE 14.2

Using an authority file (e.g., *Library of Congress name authorities*), give the correct form of the following corporate names.

a.   Department of Housing and Urban Development (located in Washington, D.C.)

b.   Market Research Department of the American Stock Exchange

c   National Clearinghouse for Family Planning Information

d.   Bureau of Vocational Information (located in New York)

e.   Faculté de médecine Saint-Antoine (part of the Université Pierre et Marie Curie)

f.   Organics Division of Imperial Chemical Industries

g. Ministry of Agriculture, Fisheries and Food (located in London)

h. National Computer Security Center (located in the United States)

i. Section of Energy and Environment of the Interstate Commerce Commission of the United States government

j. Department of Natural Resources of the Mississippi state government

EXERCISE 14.3
Find an example of:

a. a subordinate body entered under its own name (refer from parent)

_____

_____

b. a subordinate body entered under the name of its parent

_____

_____

c. a subordinate body entered indirectly under the name of its parent

_____

_____

d. a subordinate body entered under the name of a government

_____

_____

e. a government agency body entered under its own name (refer from parent)

_____

_____

f.   a subordinate body entered indirectly under the name of a government

_____

_____

MARC

Corporate names are coded in the same way as personal names, by referring to the MARC codes at the back of the book (or the USMARC manual if you have access to it). First you need to know whether the name is a main or an added entry, and then use the tag, indicators and subfield codes you need.

EXERCISE 14.4

Here are some names from Exercises 14.1 and 14.2. Code them as main entries.

a   Native Plant Society of Oregon

      110

b.   Missouri. Clean Water Commission

      110

c.   Imperial Chemical Industries. Organics Division

      110

d.   United States. Interstate Commerce Commission. Section of Energy and Environment

      110

e.   National Computer Security Center (United States)

      110

EXERCISE 14.5

Here are more names from Exercises 14.1 and 14.2. Code them as added entries.

a.   Mississippi. Dept. of Environmental Quality

      710

b.   Great Britain. Ministry of Agriculture, Fisheries and Food

      710

c.   National Underwriter Company. Reference Book Division

       710

d.   Laos

       710

e.   Music Educators National Conference (U.S.)

       710

EXERCISE 14.6

Go back to the descriptions in Chapters 7-9 which contain corporate bodies. Decide on the main and added entries, format and code them. Answers are given at the back of the book.

EXERCISE 14.7

Catalog and code the following items, including level 2 description and access points.

a.   Title page

GRAND CANYON NATIONAL PARK

COLORADO RIVER MANAGEMENT PLAN

Prepared by
Grand Canyon National Park, National Park Service,
U.S. Dept. of the Interior

U.S. DEPARTMENT OF THE INTERIOR NATIONAL PARK SERVICE
1979

Verso of the title page

© **United States Department of the Interior 1979**

ISBN 0 644 00847 4

Printed in the United States by Capitol Printing Pty. Ltd.

This booklet has 42 pages, black and white maps and photographs, and is 29.8 cm. high.

AACR2 DESCRIPTION

MARC CODING (MONOGRAPHS)

020 _____

050 _____

082 _____

1 _____

245 _____

_____

250 _____

260 _____

300 _____

4 _____

5 _____

_____

7 _____

8 _____

(This section is extracted from a standard MARC worksheet)

b.   Title page

Educational Technology Centre
Universiti Brunei Darussalam

GUIDE
TO SERVICES

Verso of the title page

Copyright © Universiti Brunei Darussalam 1996

First edition

…

Published by the:

Educational Technology Centre
Universiti Brunei Darussalam
Bandar Seri Begawan 2028
Brunei Darussalam

This booklet has 36 pages, lots of colored photographs, and is 20.5 cm. high.

AACR2 DESCRIPTION

MARC CODING (MONOGRAPHS)

020 _____

050 _____

082 _____

1 _____

245

_____

250 _____

260 _____

300 _____

4 _____

5

_____

7 _____

8 _____

(This section is extracted from a standard MARC worksheet)

Conferences, Workshops, Etc. (24.7A)

Begin with the name of the conference, without its number, frequency, date

> Conference on Ocean-Atmosphere Interaction
> *not*
> Seventh Conference on Ocean-Atmosphere Interaction

Add the number, date and place to the name

> Conference on Ocean-Atmosphere Interaction (7th : 1988 : Anaheim, Calif.)

Remember that for the proceedings of named conferences, workshops, etc., the name of the conference, etc., is the corporate body main entry of the work.

Example 1

Conference on the Medical Profession : Enduring Values and New Challenges (1987 : Los Angeles, Calif.)
Conference on the Medical Profession, Enduring Values and New Challenges : the Biltmore Hotel, Los Angeles, California, February 25-27, 1987 : proceedings. – [Chicago, Ill.] : Medical Education Group, American Medical Association, c1988. – 196 p. ; 24 cm.
Includes index.
ISBN 0 89970 316 X.
1. Medicine–Congresses. 2. Physicians–Congresses.

Example 2

CALL NUMBER:	LB1572.9 .W67 1978
AUTHOR:	World Congress on Reading (7th : 1978 : Hamburg)
TITLE:	Beginning reading instruction in different countries / Lloyd O. Ollila, editor.
PUBLISHED:	Newark, Del. : International Reading Association, c1981.
DESCRIPTION:	viii, 78 p. ; 22 cm.
SUBJECT:	Reading (Elementary)–Congresses.
SUBJECT:	Reading readiness–Congresses.
OTHER NAME:	Ollila, Lloyd O.
OTHER NAME:	Strickland, Dorothy S.
OTHER NAME:	International Reading Association.
NOTE:	"Selected papers, part 1, Seventh IRA World Congress on Reading, Hamburg, August 1–3, 1978, Dorothy S. Strickland, chairperson."
NOTE:	Includes bibliographies.
ISBN NUMBER:	0872074285
LCCN NUMBER:	80-19294

EXERCISE 14.8

Using *AACR2*, establish headings for the following. Check them in an authority file. Then code them as main entries.

a.   The Meeting of the American Anthropological Association held in San Francisco in 1992

b.   The First National Technologist Seminar held by the Faculty of Engineering, University of Dar es Salaam, 28-30 April, 1986

c.   The Oregon International Sculpture Symposium of 1974, held in Eugene, Oregon

d.   International Forum on the Indian Ocean Region held in Perth, Australia, 11-13 June 1995

e.   The 1991 Chinese Education for the 21st Century Conference held in Honolulu

EXERCISE 14.9

Catalog and code the following items, including level 2 description and access points.

a.   Cover

> # Musical Theatre in America
>
> ## Conference on the Musical Theatre in America
> ## Papers and Proceedings
>
> ## 1981
> ## C.W. Post Center

Title page

> Sponsored jointly by
> The American Society for Theatre Research
> The Sonneck Society
> The Theatre Library Association
>
> ## Musical Theatre in America
>
> Papers and Proceedings
> of the
> Conference on the Musical Theatre in America
>
> Edited by Glenn Loney
>
> Greenwood Press • Westport, Connecticut • 1984
>
> ISBN 0 3132 3524 4

Facing title page

> ## Contributions in Drama and Theater Studies
> ## Number 8
> ## ISSN 0163-3821

This book has xxi preliminary pages and 441 pages, black and white illustrations, a bibliography on pages 415 to 420, an index, and is 25 cm. high.

AACR2 DESCRIPTION

MARC CODING (MONOGRAPHS)

020 _____

050 _____

082 _____

1 _____

245 _____

_____

250 _____

260 _____

300 _____

4 _____

5 _____

_____

7 _____

8 _____

(This section is extracted from a standard MARC worksheet)

b.   Title page

**Prospects for adult education
and development
in Asia and the Pacific**

Report of a Regional Seminar
Bangkok, 24 November - 4 December 1980

UNESCO REGIONAL OFFICE FOR EDUCATION IN ASIA AND THE PACIFIC
Bangkok, Thailand, 1981

Verso of the title page

© Unesco 1981

Published by the Unesco Regional Office for Education in Asia and the Pacific
920 Sukhumvit Road
G.P.O. BOX 1425
Bangkok, Thailand

Printed in Thailand

*Opinions expressed in this publication are those of the participants of the
Regional Seminar and do not necessarily coincide with any official views of
Unesco. The designations employed and the presentation of the material herein do
not imply the expression of any opinion whatsoever on the part of Unesco
concerning the legal status of any country, or of its authorities, or concerning the
delimitations of the frontiers of any country or territory.*

This book has 69 pages, includes a list of the participants, and is 26.5 cm. high.

***AACR2* DESCRIPTION**

MARC CODING (MONOGRAPHS)

020 _____

050 _____

082 _____

1 _____

245 _____

_____

250 _____

260 _____

300 _____

4 _____

5 _____

_____

7 _____

8 _____

(This section is extracted from a standard MARC worksheet)

Chapter 15
SERIES
(CatSkill—module 20)

Introduction
A series is a collection of items which has a distinctive title although each item has its own individual title. Sometimes an item may be in more than one series.

In descriptive cataloging (at level 2 or 3), each series title must be considered in two ways:
- for the description (Rule 1.6). This must be in exactly the form in which it appears in the item
- as an access point (Rule 21.30L). Does the library want this series to be an access point in its catalog? Will readers use it as an access point?

If in doubt, make an added entry for the series.

Keep a record of all such decisions in a series authority file in order to keep entries consistent.

Series Added Entries
A series heading is the access point for the series. The series heading is usually the series title. If there are other series with the same title, extra information is added to distinguish them.

A series heading is only added as an access point if it is likely that users will search for items in the series. The cataloger decides whether to make a series added entry. Series headings are listed in name authority files like *Library of Congress name authorities.*

Types of Series
There are three kinds of series:
- Series traced exactly as in the series statement
        The world of folk dances
- Series traced differently from the series statement
        Description: Cinema heritage series, ISSN 0816-5467 ; no. 8
        Access point: Cinema heritage series
- Series not traced at all
        The modern library

Make a Series Added Entry? (21.30L1)
Make an added entry under the heading for a series if you expect that a library user will look for the item in the catalog under the series heading. It is optional to add the number in the series; in practice, very few users would search for the item under the number in the series.

In case of doubt make a series added entry.

Series Authority File

It is important to check the series authority file to:

*   see if this series heading has been already established
*   check the preferred form of the heading.

Numbered Series

Sometimes we need to trace the same heading, but without other parts of the series statement such as series numbers or the ISSN.

Not a Distinctive Series Title

Many series have titles which are not distinctive. That is, there are some series with the same title.

> Research paper
> Technical monograph

If a title like this becomes the series heading, users of the catalog will not know which series it is.

In establishing these headings, make a uniform title for the series title.

Series Uniform Titles (25.5B)

For most series like this, add the name of the corporate body responsible for the series. It can also be the place of publication, or the date, or a combination, or other identifying information.

> Technical paper (Minnesota Higher Education Coordinating Board)
> Teach yourself books (Lincolnwood, Ill.)

Series Statement Not Traced

Sometimes the series statement is not traced as a series heading. This is when the cataloger decides that the series title is not useful to any library user, and therefore should not be added to the catalog record, even though it appears in the series statement as part of the description.

EXERCISE 15.1

Use *AACR2* and LCNA to determine the headings required for the following series.

a.   Ideas in Architecture

b.   Learning local history

    c.   Imprint (a series published in Sydney, Australia)

    d.   CIRIA Research Reports

    e.   Penguin Poetry Series

    f.   Occasional paper / Pennsylvania Ethnic Heritage Studies Center

    g.   Technical bulletin of the Saskatchewan Department of Tourism and Renewable Resources

    h.   Janice S. Saunders' teach yourself to sew better series

MARC

To enter the series information in MARC format, begin with the series statement. Look again at the MARC codes for series. In order to code the series statement, decide whether the series added entry is the same as or different from the series statement, or whether there will be a series added entry at all.

If the series statement is the same as the series added entry, the coding is included in the 440 field. The tag 440 tells the computer to make a series added entry in the same form as the series statement (except that some systems leave the number in the series and the ISSN out of the heading, even if they are present in the series statement).

```
440   0   $aLearning local history
```

If there is no series added entry, the tag 490 and the first indicator 0 tell the computer not to make an added entry for the series.

```
490   0   $aPiccolo books
```

If the series added entry is different from the series statement, an additional field –
830 (Series Added Entry—Uniform Title) – is needed:

```
490   1   $aImprint
830   0   $aImprint (Sydney, N.S.W.)
```

EXERCISE 15.2

Code the following series statements and series headings.

a. Series statement: Learning local history

Series heading: Learning local history

440

b. Series statement: Penguin poetry

Series heading: None - series not traced

490

c. Series statement: Occasional paper / Pennsylvania Ethnic Heritage Studies Center

490

Series heading: Occasional paper (Pennsylvania Ethnic Heritage Studies Center)

830

d. Series statement: Technical bulletin / Saskatchewan. Dept. of Tourism and Renewable Resources

490

Series heading: Technical bulletin (Saskatchewan. Dept. of Tourism and Renewable Resources)

830

EXERCISE 15.3
Catalog and code the following item, including level 2 description and access points.

Title page

**Disadvantaged Post-Adolescents:
Approaches to Education and
Rehabilitation**

REUVEN KOHEN-RAZ
The Hebrew University

GORDON	AND	BREACH	SCIENCE	PUBLISHERS
New York	London	Paris	Montreux	Tokyo

Facing title page

Special Aspects of Education
A series of books edited by Roy Evans, Roehampton Institute, London, UK, and
Herman Green, Northern Illinois University, De Kalb, Illinois, USA.

Volume 1
Disadvantaged Post-Adolescents:
Approaches to Education and
Rehabilitation
Reuven Kohen-Raz

Volume 2
Israelis in Institutions:
Studies in Child Placement, Practice and Policy
Eliezer D. Jaffe

ISSN: 0731-8413

Verso of the title page

Copyright © 1983 by Gordon and Breach, Science Publishers, Inc.

Gordon and Breach, Science Publishers, Inc.
One Park Avenue
New York, NY 10016

…

ISBN 0-677-06010-6, ISSN 0731-8413. Printed in Great Britain.

This book has diagrams and tables of numbers, is 23.5 cm. high, and has xii preliminary pages and 224
pages of text, including a bibliography on pages 202 to 211 and an index.

AACR2 DESCRIPTION

MARC CODING (MONOGRAPHS)

020 _____

050 _____

082 _____

1 _____

245 _____

_____

250 _____

260 _____

300 _____

4 _____

5 _____

_____

7 _____

8 _____

(This section is extracted from a standard MARC worksheet)

Chapter 16
UNIFORM TITLES
(CatSkill—module 21)

Introduction
There are two kinds of uniform titles, which serve apparently opposite purposes:
*   for monographs, a uniform title brings together all the versions of a work, so that library users can find all the versions under one heading
    e.g., Bible
*   for serials and series, a uniform title distinguishes between identical titles
    e.g., Monograph (Kansas Agricultural Experiment Station).

The use of uniform titles depends on the policy of the cataloging agency. Many libraries do not use uniform titles.

Uniform title and name-title headings are included in name authority files.

Uniform Titles for Monographs
Use a uniform title for a monograph when:
*   the work has appeared under different titles proper
    e.g., Mark Twain's work *The adventures of Huckleberry Finn* is also issued under the title *Huckleberry Finn*
*   translations need to be kept together with the original work
    e.g., Gabriel García Márquez's *Love in the time of cholera* is an English translation of *Amor en los tiempos del cólera*
*   the title of the work is obscured by the wording of the title proper
    e.g., Dickens' *Dealings with the firm of Dombey and son, wholesale, retail and for exportation* is really *Dombey and son.*

Chapter 25
The rules for uniform titles are contained in Chapter 25 of *AACR2*. A brief summary of the most important rules is included here. You will need to consult the rules themselves for details and examples.

Use of a uniform title depends on:
*   how well the work is known
*   how many manifestations of the work are involved
*   whether another work with the same title proper has been identified
*   whether the main entry is under title
*   whether the work was originally in another language
*   the extent to which the catalog is used for research purposes.

General Rule

In general, the best known English title of a work is chosen as the uniform title. It is usually enclosed in square brackets, and given before the title proper.

[Bible]

Translation (25.5C1)

The uniform title includes the original title and the language of the item being cataloged.

[Amor en los tiempos del cólera. English]

Collective Titles

25.8A. Use the collective title *Works* for an item that consists of ... the complete works of a person ...

Shakespeare, William, ...
[Works]
The complete works of Shakespeare

25.9A. Use the collective title *Selections* for items consisting of three or more works in various forms, or in one form if the person created works in one form only, and for items consisting of extracts, etc., from the works of one person.

Whitman, Walt
[Selections]
Selections from Walt Whitman and Emily Dickinson

25.10A. Use one of the following collective titles for an item ...
Correspondence
Essays
Novels
Plays
Poems
Prose works
Short stories
Speeches

Whitman, Walt
[Selections]
Collected poetry

Whitman, Walt
[Poems. Selections]
Selections from *Song of myself* and other poems

Special Rules

Chapter 25 gives details of certain types of work which use uniform titles. These include:

    manuscripts
    laws
    treaties
    sacred scriptures
    liturgical works
    musical works.

If you need these uniform titles, refer to Chapter 25 or a name authority file.

Works Entered under Title (25.2E1)

If a work is entered under a uniform title, make an added entry under the title proper of the item being cataloged.

For example, the book *A thousand and one nights* is entered under the uniform title *Arabian nights*. Therefore an added entry is given to the title proper *A thousand and one nights*.

Works Entered under Name (25.2E2)

If a work is entered under a personal or corporate heading and a uniform title is used, make an added entry under the title proper of the item being cataloged.

For example, here is a book translated into German from English. Enter it under the personal name followed by the uniform title, and then the title proper.

> Koch, C. J. (Christopher John), 1932-
> [Year of living dangerously. German].
> Ein Jahr in der Hölle

Make an added entry for the title proper, i.e., *Ein Jahr in der Hölle*.

Check the Authority File

As with other headings, check an authority file after you have constructed your heading according to the *AACR2* rules.

MARC

Many libraries do not use uniform titles, so they are treated only briefly here. The coding for a uniform title follows the same principles as the coding of names.

EXERCISE 16.1

Using *AACR2* and an authority file, provide and code a uniform title for each of the following:

a.   Mother Goose nursery rhymes

130

b.   Shakespeare, William. The tragedy of Macbeth

100

240

c.   The song of Roland

130

d.   The song of Solomon

130

e.   Book of the thousand nights and a night

130

f.   The Dead Sea scriptures in English translation

130

g.   La livre de Mormon

130

EXERCISE 16.2

Catalog and code the following item, including level 2 description and access points.

Title page

EMILY DICKINSON

————

SELECTED POEMS

New York • St. Martin's Press • 1993

Verso of the title page

Originally published in the United Kingdom
First U.S. edition, published in the United States by St Martin's Press
1993

© Emily Dickinson

ISBN 0 3120 9752 2 (hardcover)

Printed in the United States of America

Front and back covers

BLOOMSBURY POETRY CLASSICS

This book is 16 cm. high and has xvi preliminary pages and 128 pages of text, including an index.

AACR2 DESCRIPTION

MARC CODING (MONOGRAPHS)

020 _____

050 _____

082 _____

1 _____

245 _____

_____

250 _____

260 _____

300 _____

4 _____

5 _____

_____

7 _____

8 _____

(This section is extracted from a standard MARC worksheet)

Uniform Titles for Serials

Use a uniform title for a serial to distinguish it from another serial with the same title proper.

For example, there are many serials called *Bulletin* or *Newsletter*. To identify each individual serial, a qualifier is added after the title proper.

> Bulletin (Columbia Society of International Law)
> Bulletin (Sydney, N.S.W.)

Qualifiers

25.5B. Add in parentheses an appropriate explanatory word, brief phrase, or other designation to distinguish a uniform title used as a heading ... from an identical or similar uniform title used as a heading or reference.

In other words, add to the title proper something in parentheses which will distinguish it from other serials with the same title.

Select from the following:
a)   place of publication
b)   corporate body
c)   place and date; or corporate body and date
d)   date
e)   edition statement, other title information, etc.

For example:
> Forum (Zagreb, Croatia)
> Bulletin (Confederation nationale des cadres du Quebec)
> New broadside (New York, N.Y. : 1970)
> Newsletter (Ontario Bird Banding Association : 1997)
> Broadside (1909)

Check an Authority File

As with other headings, it is wise to check in an authority file. Uniform titles for serials are usually found in a name authority file, e.g., *Library of Congress name authorities*.

EXERCISE 16.3

Using an authority file, provide and code a uniform title for each of the following serials.

1.   Newsletter, published by the Louisiana Historical Association

2.   Forum : the independent daily of the NGO Forum on Women, Beijing '95

      130

3.   The Bulletin, issued by the Department of Labor of the State of New York

      130

4.   Forum, published in Carlisle, Pennsylvania

      130

5.   The Newsletter of the Ontario Forestry Association, first published 1997

      130

Chapter 17
CATALOGING PROCEDURES

The Cataloging Process

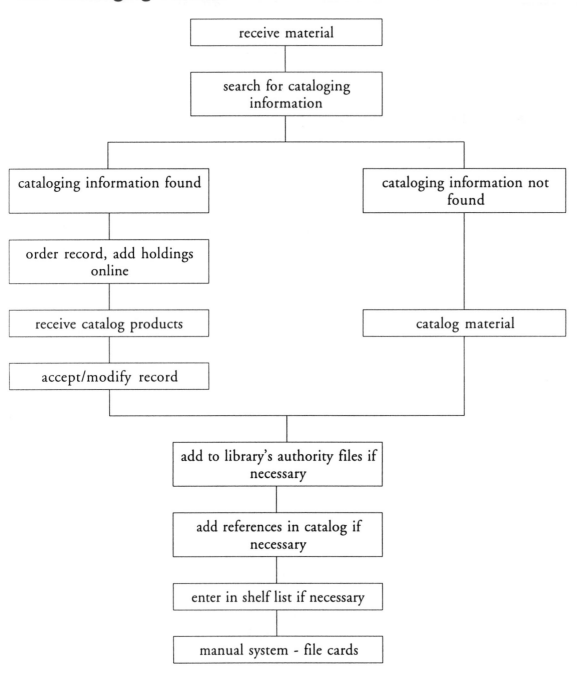

receive material

search for cataloging information

cataloging information found

cataloging information not found

order record, add holdings online

receive catalog products

catalog material

accept/modify record

add to library's authority files if necessary

add references in catalog if necessary

enter in shelf list if necessary

manual system - file cards

Sources of Catalog Copy

There are many sources of cataloging copy. These range from exchanging records within a coperative network to purchasing catalog records, either in hard or electronic copy from commercial suppliers. Some library suppliers provide records with the items when they are purchased. There are also companies from whom retrospective records are available.

Cataloging-in-Publication (CIP)

Cataloging-in-Publication is usually printed in the work. This means that it is created before the work is published, and often before it is completed.

Since changes can occur between creation of the CIP and publication, and the cataloger usually does not see the completed work, it is less reliable cataloging copy than a record from an established cataloging source.

It is also incomplete, since it does not contain publication and physical description details. However it is still valuable, especially if no other records are readily available.

Using Cataloging Copy

- Check that the cataloging copy and the item in hand are the same.
- Check the correctness of the copy:
  - descriptive cataloging
  - classification number
  - subject headings
- Accept the copy; or modify it to suit the needs of your library.

Buying Catalog Cards

If catalog cards are acquired, it is rarely cost-effective to alter them, other than to add your library's call number to each card. They must then be filed in the catalog according to the heading, and the additional main entry card in the shelf list by the call number. It is useful to mark the shelf list card with, for example, "S.L." to avoid confusion with the catalog cards.

Problems / Errors Found in Copy Cataloging

The following are among the most common errors to watch for:

- transcription errors, e.g., misspelling, punctuation, number of pages
- missing information, e.g., areas of description, elements of description, added entries
- outdated copy, e.g., *AACR1*
- differences relating to local holdings, e.g.,
  - multivolume works—the library may have only partial holdings
  - different publisher, all the other information is the same.

EXERCISE 17.1

What's wrong with this copy?

a.

738.0977191
Purviance, Lousie
Zanesville art poetry in color / by Louise and Evan Purviance. – Leon, Iowa : Mid-America Book Co., 1968.
50 p. : col. ill. ; 23 cm.

1. Pottery – Zanesville, Ohio – Catalogs. I. Purvinace, Evan. II. Title

b.

582.0014
Plowden, C. Chicheley
A manual of plant names / by C. Chichley Plowden. – 3rd ed. – London : Allen and Unwin, 1972.
260 p. : ill. ; 23 cm. – (British Museum series on botany)
Includes index.

1. Botany – Nomenclature. I. Title.

c.

HL536.7S56
South of the Sahara : development in African economics. Edited by Sayre P. Schatz. Philadelphia, Temple University Press, [1972].
vii, 363 p. 23 cm. $10.00
Includes bibliographic references.

1. Africa, Sub-Sahara – Economic conditions I. Schatz, Sayre P. ed.

d.

629.13
Dwiggins, Don
The sky is yours : you and the world of flight. – Washington, D.C. : Children's Press, [1983].
p.

Explores the many careers & hobbies open in general aviation.
1. Aeronautics as a profession. I Title.

e.   See the title page on the next page for which this is the record:

030
Whittaker, Kenneth
Dictionaries / Kenneth Whittaker. – London : The Library Association, 1986.
88 p. ; 20 cm. – (The readers guide series)

1. Encyclopedias and dictionaries. I. Title. II. Series.

```
┌─────────────────────────────────────────────────────────────┐
│                                                               │
│                        (TITLE PAGE)                           │
│                                                               │
│       the reader's guide series : editor K. C. Harrison       │
│                                                               │
│                        DICTIONARIES                           │
│                                                               │
│                     Kenneth Whittaker                         │
│                                                               │
│                                                               │
│          JAMES BENNETT       LANHAM, MD.                      │
│                          1986                                 │
│                                                               │
│                                                               │
│            [Additional information from book                  │
│                        88 pages                               │
│                     20.1 cm. high]                            │
│                                                               │
└─────────────────────────────────────────────────────────────┘
```

Procedure for Adding Extra Copies

- Check the catalog for the exact record.
- Check the item to ensure it is not a new edition.
- Write the call number in the appropriate position on the item.
- Add the number of copies to the automated system (or shelf list in a manual system).
- Send the item for processing.

Creating Catalog Cards

If your library produces its own catalog cards, begin by creating a main entry card, with a main entry heading, description and tracings. Add subject headings and a call number.

Make the required number of copies of this card—one for each tracing, plus one for the shelf list. Add one heading to the top of each card, and mark the shelf list card with, for example, "S.L." to avoid confusion with the catalog cards.

For title added entry cards (i.e., if the tracing is "Title"), add only the title proper to the top of the card (Rule 21.30J1).

For series added entry cards when the series is traced the same (i.e., if the tracing is "Series"), add the series title exactly as it appears in the series statement. For series added entry cards when the series is traced differently (e.g., if the tracing is "Series: Library education series (Lanham, Md.)"), add the series heading given in the tracing.

For all other added entry and subject cards, add the heading exactly as given in the tracing.

File the catalog cards alphabetically according to the heading, and the shelf list card numerically by the call number.

EXERCISE 17.2

Here is a set of main entry cards. Create catalog and shelf list cards by adding an appropriate heading or label to each card.

746.46
LID

Liddell, Jill

The patchwork pilgrimage : how to create vibrant church decorations
and vestments with quilting techniques / Jill Liddell ; with historical
essays by Andrew Liddell. - New York : Viking Studio Books, c1993.
vii, 172 p. : ill. (some col.) ; 29 cm.
Includes bibliographical references (p. 172)
ISBN 0525936890

    I. Liddell, Andrew II. Title 1. Patchwork

746.46
LID

Liddell, Jill

The patchwork pilgrimage : how to create vibrant church decorations
and vestments with quilting techniques / Jill Liddell ; with historical
essays by Andrew Liddell. - New York : Viking Studio Books, c1993.
vii, 172 p. : ill. (some col.) ; 29 cm.
Includes bibliographical references (p. 172)
ISBN 0525936890

    I. Liddell, Andrew II. Title 1. Patchwork

746.46
LID

Liddell, Jill

The patchwork pilgrimage : how to create vibrant church decorations
and vestments with quilting techniques / Jill Liddell ; with historical
essays by Andrew Liddell. - New York : Viking Studio Books, c1993.
vii, 172 p. : ill. (some col.) ; 29 cm.
Includes bibliographical references (p. 172)
ISBN 0525936890

    I. Liddell, Andrew II. Title 1. Patchwork

```
                                                        746.46
                                                        LID

    Liddell, Jill

    The patchwork pilgrimage : how to create vibrant church decorations
    and vestments with quilting techniques / Jill Liddell ; with historical
    essays by Andrew Liddell. - New York : Viking Studio Books, c1993.
    vii, 172 p. : ill. (some col.) ; 29 cm.
    Includes bibliographical references (p. 172)
    ISBN 0525936890

    I. Liddell, Andrew  II. Title  1. Patchwork
```

```
                                                        746.46
                                                        LID

    Liddell, Jill

    The patchwork pilgrimage : how to create vibrant church decorations
    and vestments with quilting techniques / Jill Liddell ; with historical
    essays by Andrew Liddell. - New York : Viking Studio Books, c1993.
    vii, 172 p. : ill. (some col.) ; 29 cm.
    Includes bibliographical references (p. 172)
    ISBN 0525936890

    I. Liddell, Andrew  II. Title  1. Patchwork
```

Levels of Cataloging Work

Until quite recently, original cataloging was regarded as a professional activity in libraries—that is, it was done by qualified librarians, and library technicians usually did copy cataloging and catalog maintenance.

This situation is changing: catalogs are being automated and the skills of library technicians are increasingly recognized.

Libraries also differ, and individual interests and skills as well as the pressures of work are factors in the allocation of responsibilities.

Cataloging Activities

EXERCISE 17.3

Put a tick next to each activity listed which is performed in libraries by the level of person specified. You will find that many activities are carried out by more than one level of staff.

ACTIVITIES	Librarian	Library Technician	Clerical Assistant	P/T Help (e.g., students)
1. Establishes policies and procedures				
2. Supervision				
3. Does original cataloging				
4. Performs bibliographic checking for main entries				
5. Solves difficult bibliographic checking problems				
6. Catalogs material with cataloging information available				
7. Locates records in computer-based network				
8. Does descriptive and subject cataloging on problem material				
9. Checks cataloging				
10. Catalogs by comparing with existing catalog records				
11. Checks cataloging using existing catalog records				
12. Enters cataloging data				
13. Checks entry of cataloging data				
14. Reproduces shelf list cards				
15. Files in shelf list				
16. Checks shelf list filing				
17. Supervises data entry and regulates workload				
18. Prepares books for circulation				
19. Supervises book preparation				
20. Maintains authority files				

REVISION QUIZ 17.4

Use the following questions to revise your understanding of cataloging procedures. You do not need to write down all the answers.

a.   List 5 physical forms of a catalog.

      i.

      ii.

      iii.

      iv.

      v.

b.   Which forms do you think are best from a user's point of view? Explain.

c.   Automated catalogs have the possibility of providing much more information than manual ones. Give two examples of this.

      i.

      ii.

d.   What is the difference between original cataloging and copy cataloging?

e.   What is centralized cataloging? Give an example.

f. List 3 advantages of centralized cataloging.

    i.

    ii.

    iii.

g. List 3 disadvantages of centralized cataloging.

    i.

    ii.

    iii.

h. List 3 advantages of cooperative cataloging.

    i.

    ii.

    iii.

i. List 3 disadvantages of cooperative cataloging.

    i.

    ii.

    iii.

j. List 3 ways of obtaining records for copy cataloging.

    i.

    ii.

    iii.

k. List tasks library technicians may perform in a cataloging department.

    i.

    ii.

    iii.

      iv.

      v.

      vi.

l.   Library staff are usually organized into two major divisions. What are they called?

      i.

      ii.

m.   To which division does the cataloging department belong?

n.   The library catalog can be said to be the link between the above two divisions. Explain how each division relates to the catalog.

o.   Give three reasons why browsing on the shelves is an inadequate way of finding out what is in a library.

      i.

      ii.

      iii.

p.   What is a union catalog? Give an example, and explain one use.

q.   List the basic steps needed to get a book into circulation in a library.

r.   Explain briefly 2 ways in which a knowledge of cataloging helps in other areas of library work.

MARC CODES

The *MARC21 Concise Format for Bibliographic Data* is available on the Internet at http://lcweb.loc.gov/marc/bibliographic/ecbdhome.html

020 INTERNATIONAL STANDARD BOOK NUMBER (R)

Indicators
Both undefined; each contains a blank (#)

Subfield Codes
$a   International Standard Book Number (NR)
$c   Terms of availability (NR)
$z   Cancelled/invalid ISBN (R)

Example
020   ## $a087779001X (cased) :$c$12.50

022 INTERNATIONAL STANDARD SERIAL NUMBER (R)

Indicators
First Level of international interest
    #   Level of international interest not designated (used by all institutions other than the National Serials Data Program (NSDP) and ISDS/Canada)
    0   Serial of international interest; full record registered with ISSN network (used only by National Serials Data Program (NSDP) and ISDS/Canada)
    1   Serial not of international interest; abbreviated record registered with ISSN network
Second Undefined; contains a blank (#)

Subfield Codes
$a   International Standard Serial Number (NR)
$y   Incorrect ISSN (R)
$z   Cancelled ISSN (R)

Example
022   ## $a1224-9495

050 - LIBRARY OF CONGRESS CALL NUMBER (R)

Indicators
First Existence in LC collection
    #   No information provided
    0   Item is in LC
    1   Item is not in LC
Second Source of call number
    0   Assigned by LC
    4   Assigned by agency other than LC

Subfield Codes
$a   Classification number (R)
$b   Item number (NR
$3   Materials specified (NR)

Examples
050   #4 $aNB933.F44 $bT6
050   10 $aBJ1533.C4 $bL49
050   00 $aJK609 $b.M2
050   00 $aZ7164.N3 $bL34 no. 9 $aZ7165.R42 $aHC517.R42

082   DEWEY DECIMAL CALL NUMBER (R)

Indicators
First Type of edition
       0   Full edition
       1   Abridged edition
Second Source of call number
       0   Assigned by LC
       4   Assigned by agency other than LC

Subfield Codes
$a   Classification (R)
$b   Item number (NR)
$2   Edition number (NR)

Example
082   00 $a330.965$221

100   MAIN ENTRY - PERSONAL NAME (NR)

Indicators
First Type of personal name entry element
       0   Forename
       1   Surname
       3   Family name
Second Undefined; contains a blank (#)

Subfield Codes
$a   Personal name (NR)
$b   Numeration (Roman numerals used in the entry element of the name) (NR)
$c   Titles and other words associated with the name (R)
$d   Dates associated with the name (NR)
$e   Relator term (R)
$f   Date of a work (NR)
$g   Miscellaneous information (NR)
$k   Form subheading (R)
$l   Language of a work (NR)
$n   Number of section/part of a work (R)

$p   Name of section/part of a work (R)
$q   Fuller form of name (NR)
$t   Title of work (NR)

Examples
100   0# $aAlexander$b1, $cEmperor of Russia.
100   1# $aLawrence, D. H. $q(David Herbert)
100   1# $aal-Shaykh, Hanan,$d1945-

110   MAIN ENTRY - CORPORATE NAME (NR)
Indicators
First Type of corporate name entry element
       0   Inverted name
       1   Jurisdiction name
       2   Name in direct order
Second Undefined; contains a blank (#)

Subfield Codes
$a   Corporate name or jurisdiction name as entry element (NR)
$b   Subordinate unit (R)
$c   Location of meeting (NR)
$d   Date of meeting or treaty signing (R)
$e   Relator term (R)
$f   Date of a work (NR)
$g   Miscellaneous information (NR)
$k   Form subheading (R)
$l   Language of a work (NR)
$n   Number of section/part of meeting (R)
$p   Name of section/part of meeting (R)
$t   Title of work

Examples
110   1# $aUnited States.$bDept. of Agriculture.
110   2# $aSt. James Church (Bronx, New York, N.Y.)

111   MAIN ENTRY - MEETING NAME (NR)
Indicators
First Type of meeting name entry element
       0   Inverted name
       1   Jurisdiction name
       2   Name in direct order
Second Undefined; contains a blank (#)

Subfield Codes
$a   Meeting name or jurisdiction name as entry element (NR)
$c   Location of meeting (NR)
$d   Date of meeting (R)
$e   Subordinate unit (R)

$f   Date of a work (NR)
$g   Miscellaneous information (NR)
$k   Form subheading (R)
$l   Language of a work (NR)
$n   Number of section/part of meeting (R)
$p   Name of section/part of meeting (R)
$q   Name of meeting following jurisdiction name entry element (NR)
$t   Title of work

Example
111   2# $aLabour Party (Great Britain).$eConference ($n71st :$cBlackpool, Lancashire)

130   MAIN ENTRY - UNIFORM TITLE (NR)

A uniform title used as a main entry in a bibliographic record.

Indicators
First Nonfiling characters
        0-9 Number of nonfiling characters present
Second Undefined; contains a blank (#)

Subfield Codes
$a   Uniform title (NR)
$d   Date of treaty signing (R)
$f   Date of a work (NR)
$g   Miscellaneous information (NR)
$h   Medium (NR)
$k   Form subheading (R)
$l   Language of a work (NR)
$m   Medium of performance for music (R)
$n   Number of section/part of a work (R)
$o   Arranged statement for music (NR)
$p   Name of section/part of a work (R)
$r   Key for music (NR)
$s   Version (NR)
$t   Title of a work (NR)

Examples
130   0# $aGenesis (Old Saxon poem)
130   0# $aReynard the fox. $lFrench.
130   0# $aBible. $pN.T. $pMatthew. $lEnglish. $f1976.

240   UNIFORM TITLE (NR)

The uniform title for an item when the bibliographic description is entered under a main entry field that contains a personal (field 100), corporate (110), or meeting (111) name. The brackets that customarily enclose a uniform title are not carried in the USMARC record. They may be generated based on the field tag.

Indicators

First Uniform title printed or displayed
    0   Not printed or displayed
    1   Printed or displayed
Second Nonfiling characters
    0-9 Number of nonfiling characters present

Subfield Codes
$a   Uniform title (NR)
$d   Date of treaty signing (R)
$f   Date of a work (NR)
$g   Miscellaneous information (NR)
$h   Medium (NR)
$k   Form subheading (R)
$l   Language of a work (NR)
$m   Medium of performance for music (R)
$n   Number of section/part of a work (R)
$o   Arranged statement for music (NR)
$p   Name of section/part of a work (R)
$r   Key for music (NR)
$s   Version (NR)

Examples
240 10 $aGenesis (Old Saxon poem)
240 10 $aReynard the fox. $lFrench.
240 10 $aBible. $pN.T. $pMatthew. $lEnglish. $f1976.

245 TITLE STATEMENT (NR)
Indicators
First Title added entry
    0   No title added entry
    1   Title added entry
Second Nonfiling characters
    0-9 Number of nonfiling characters present

Subfield Codes
$a   Title (R)
$b   Remainder of title (NR)
$c   Remainder of title page transcription/statement of responsibility (NR)
$f   Inclusive dates (NR)
$g   Bulk dates (NR)
$h   Medium (NR)
$k   Form (R)
$n   Number of part/section of a work (R)
$p   Name of part/section of a work (R)
$s   Version (NR)

Examples
245 04 $aThe essentials of chemistry /$cedited by J.Barker.
245 10 $aKaro :$bthe life and fate of a Papuan /$cAmirah Inglis.

246 VARYING FORM OF TITLE (R)

Indicators
First Note controller/title added entry
   0 Note, no title added entry
   1 Note, title added entry
   2 No note, no title added entry
   3 No note, title added entry
Second Type of title
   # No information provided
   0 Portion of title
   1 Parallel title
   2 Distinctive title
   3 Other title
   4 Cover title
   5 Added title page title
   6 Caption title
   7 Running title
   8 Spine title

Subfield Codes
$a Title proper/short title (NR)
$b Remainder of title (NR)
$f Designation of volume and issue number and/or date of a work (NR)
$g Miscellaneous information (NR)
$h Medium (NR)
$i Display text (NR)
$n Number of part/section of a work (R)
$p Name of part/section of a work (R)

Examples
245 14 $aThe Macintosh bible.
246 1# $aMac bible

250 EDITION STATEMENT (NR)

Indicators
Both undefined; each contains a blank (#)

Subfield Codes
$a Edition statement proper (NR)
$b Remainder of edition statement (NR)

Examples
250 ## $a3rd. ed.

250 ## $aRev. ed. /$brevised by Susan Smith.

254   MUSICAL PRESENTATION STATEMENT (NR)

Indicators
Both undefined; each contains a blank (#)

Subfield Codes
$a   Musical presentation statement

Example
254 ## $aScore and set of parts.

255   CARTOGRAPHIC MATHEMATICAL DATA (R)

Indicators
Both undefined; each contains a blank (#)

Subfield Codes
$a   Statement of scale (NR)
$b   Statement of projection (NR)
$c   Statement of coordinates (NR)
$d   Statement of zone (NR)
$e   Statement of equinox (NR)

Example
255 ## $aScales differ.

256   COMPUTER FILE CHARACTERISTICS (NR)

Indicators
Both undefined; each contains a blank (#)

Subfield Codes
$a   Computer file characteristics (NR)

Example
256 ## $aComputer data (2 files : 860 000, 775 000 records).

260   PUBLICATION, DISTRIBUTION, ETC. (IMPRINT) (NR)

Indicators
Both undefined; each contains a blank (#)

Subfield Codes
$a   Place of publication, distribution, etc. (R)
$b   Name of publisher, distributor, etc. (R)
$c   Date of publication, distribution, etc. (R)

$e   Place of manufacture (NR)
$f   Manufacturer (NR)
$g   Date of manufacture (NR)

Examples
260 ## $aNew York :$bWiley,$c1987.
260 ## $aLondon ;$aMelbourne :$bVintage,$c1991.
260 ## $aLondon :$bSouvenir Press ;$aToronto :$bDent,$c1972.

300   PHYSICAL DESCRIPTION (R)

Indicators
Both undefined; each contains a blank (#)

Subfield Codes
$a   Extent of item (R)
$b   Other physical details (NR)
$c   Dimensions (R)
$e   Accompanying material (NR)
$f   Type of unit (R)
$g   Size of unit (R)

Examples
300 ## $axxi, 265 p. :$bill. ;$c24 cm.
300 ## $a266 slides :$bcol. ;$c5 x 5 cm. +$e1 guide.

310   CURRENT PUBLICATION FREQUENCY (NR)

Indicators
Both undefined; each contains a blank (#)

Subfield Codes
$a   Current publication frequency (NR)
$b   Date of current publication frequency (NR)

Example
310 ## $aWeekly

362   DATES OF PUBLICATION AND/OR VOLUME DESIGNATION (R)

Indicators
First Format of date
     0   Formatted style (i.e., dates appear in this area)
     1   Unformatted note (i.e., dates appear in the notes area)
Second Undefined; contains a blank (#)

Subfield Codes
$a   Dates of publication and/or sequential designation (NR)
$z   Source of information (NR)

Example
362 0# $aIssue no. 1 (Jan./Mar. 1982)-

440 SERIES STATEMENT/ADDED ENTRY - TITLE (R)

This field is used when the series statement is the same as the series added entry. In some systems, this may include a number and/or ISSN which appears in the series statement, but which the system automatically omits from the series heading.

Indicators
First Undefined; contains a blank (#)
Second Nonfiling characters
    0-9 Number of nonfiling characters present

Subfield Codes
$a   Title (NR)
$n   Number of part/section of a work (R)
$p   Name of part/section of a work (R)
$v   Volume number/sequential designation (NR)
$x   ISSN (NR)

Examples
440 #0 $aStudies in biological science
440 #4 $aThe pediatric clinics of North America ;$vv. 2, no. 4

490 SERIES STATEMENT (R)

This field is used when the series statement is different from the series added entry, or when there is a series statement in the description, but a series added entry is not required.

Indicators
First   Specifies whether series is traced
    0   Series not traced
    1   Series traced differently
Second Undefined; contains a blank (#)

Subfield Codes
$a   Series statement (R)
$l   Library of Congress call number (NR)
$v   Volume number/sequential designation (R)
$x   ISSN (NR)

Examples
490 0# $aLife series ;$vv. 6

490 1# $aPolicy series/CES ;$v1
830 #0 $aPolicy series (Centre for Environment Studies (London, England)) ;$v1

500 GENERAL NOTE (R)

Indicators
Both undefined; each contains a blank (#)

Subfield Codes
$a   General note (NR)

Example
500   ## $aIncludes index.

501 WITH NOTE (R)

Indicators
Both undefined; each contains a blank (#)

Subfield Codes
$a   With note (NR)

Example
501   ## $aWith (on verso): Motor road map of south-east Victoria.

504 BIBLIOGRAPHY, ETC. NOTE (R)

Indicators
Both undefined; each contains a blank (#)

Subfield Codes
$a   Bibliography, etc. note (NR)
$b   Number of references (NR)

Example
504   ## $aBibliography: p. 238-239.

505 FORMATTED CONTENTS NOTE (NR)

Indicators
First   Display constant controller
       0   Contents
       1   Incomplete contents
       2   Partial contents
       8   No display constant generated
Second Level of content designation
       #   Basic
       0   Enhanced

Subfield Codes
$a   Formatted contents note (NR)
$g   Miscellaneous information (R)

$r   Statement of responsibility (R)
$t   Title (R)

Example
505   0# $aTriple concerto in C major, Op. 56 / Beethoven - Double concerto in A minor, Op. 102 / Brahms.

508   CREATION/PRODUCTION CREDITS NOTE (NR)
Indicators
Both undefined; each contains a blank (#)

Subfield Codes
$a   Creation/production credits note (NR)

Example
508   ## $aProducer: Michelle Lewis.

511   PARTICIPANT OR PERFORMER NOTE (R)
Indicators
First   Display constant controller
        0   No display constant generated
        1   Cast
Second   Undefined; contains a blank (#)

Subfield Codes
$a   Participant or performer note (NR)

Example
511   0# $aNarrator: Richard Burton.

516   TYPE OF COMPUTER FILE OR DATA NOTE (R)
Indicators
First   Display constant controller
        #   No information provided
        8   No display constant generated
Second   Undefined; contains a blank (#)

Subfield Codes
$a   Type of computer file or data note (NR)

Example
516   ## $aProgram and data.

520 SUMMARY, ETC. NOTE (R)

Indicators

First   Display constant controller

      #   No information provided

      0   Subject

      1   Review

      8   No display constant generated

Second Undefined; contains a blank (#)

Subfield Codes

$a   Summary, etc. note (NR)

$b   Expansion of summary note (NR)

Example

520 0# $aDescribes Mexico's Museum of Anthropology as one of the great museums of the world.

521 TARGET AUDIENCE NOTE (R)

Indicators

First   Display constant controller

      #   No information provided

      0   Reading grade level

      1   Interest age level

      2   Interest grade level

      3   Special audience characteristics

      4   Motivation/interest level

      8   No display constant generated

Second Undefined; contains a blank (#)

Subfield Codes

$a   Target audience note (NR)

$b   Source (NR)

Example

521 0# $a10 years and up.

538 SYSTEM DETAILS NOTE (R)

Indicators

Both undefined; each contains a blank (#)

Subfield Codes

$a   System details note (NR)

Example

538 ## $aSystem requirements: Macintosh System 7 or higher, 5 Mb RAM, color monitor.

546 LANGUAGE NOTE (R)

Indicators
Both undefined; each contains a blank (#)

Subfield Codes
$a Language note (NR)
$b Information code or alphabet (R)

Example
546 ## $aFrench dialogue, English subtitles.

600 SUBJECT ADDED ENTRY - PERSONAL NAME (R)

A subject added entry in which the entry element is a personal name.

Indicators
First Type of personal name entry element
    0 Forename
    1 Surname
    3 Family name
Second Subject heading system/thesaurus
    0 Library of Congress Subject Headings/LC authority files
    1 LC subject headings for children's literature
    2 Medical Subject Headings/NLM authority files
    3 National Agricultural Library subject authority file
    4 Source not specified
    5 Canadian Subject Headings/NLC authority file
    6 Repertoire des vedettes-matiere/NLC authority file

Subfield Codes
$a Personal name (NR)
$b Numeration (NR)
$c Titles and other words associated with a name (R)
$d Dates associated with a name (NR)
$e Relator term (R)
$f Date of a work (NR)
$g Miscellaneous information (NR)
$h Medium (NR)
$k Form subheading (R)
$l Language of a work (NR)
$n Number of part/section of a work (R)
$p Name of part/section of a work (R)
$q Fuller form of name (NR)
$s Version (NR)
$t Title of a work (NR)
$v Form subdivision (R)
$x General subdivision (R)
$y Chronological subdivision (R)
$z Geographic subdivision (R)

Examples

600 00 $aNorodom Sihanouk, $cPrince, $d1922-

600 30 $aDunlop family.

600 10 $aDrake, Francis, $cSir, $d1540?-1596.

600 10 $aShakespeare, William, $d1564-1616. $tHamlet.

600 10 $aShakespeare, William, $d1564-1616 $xCriticism and interpretation $xHistory $y18th century.

600 10 $aPushkin, Aleksandr Sergeevich, $d1799-1837 $xMuseums, relics, etc. $zRussia (Federation) $zMoscow $vMaps.

600 10 $aNixon, Richard M. $q(Richard Milhouse), $d1913-1994$xPersonality.

610 SUBJECT ADDED ENTRY - CORPORATE NAME (R)

A subject added entry in which the entry element is a corporate name.

Indicators

First   Type of corporate name entry element

    0   Inverted name

    1   Jurisdiction name

    2   Name in direct order

Second   Subject heading system/thesaurus

    0   Library of Congress Subject Headings/LC authority files

    1   LC subject headings for children's literature

    2   Medical Subject Headings/NLM authority files

    3   National Agricultural Library subject authority file

    4   Source not specified

    5   Canadian Subject Headings/NLC authority file

    6   Repertoire des vedettes-matiere/NLC authority file

Subfield Codes

$a   Corporate name or jurisdiction name as entry element (NR)

$b   Subordinate unit (R)

$c   Location of meeting (NR)

$d   Date of meeting or treaty signing (R)

$e   Relator term (R)

$f   Date of a work (NR)

$g   Miscellaneous information (NR)

$h   Medium (NR)

$k   Form subheading (R)

$l   Language of a work (NR)

$n   Number of part/section/meeting (R)

$p   Name of part/section of a work (R)

$r   Key for music (NR)

$s   Version (NR)

$t   Title of a work (NR)

$v   Form subdivision (R)

$x   General subdivision (R)

$y   Chronological subdivision (R)

$z   Geographic subdivision (R)

Examples
610 20 $aEmpire State Building (New York, N.Y.)
610 10 $aGreat Britain. $tTreaties, etc. $gIreland, $d1985 Nov. 15.
610 20 $aBritish Library. $kManuscript. $nArundel 384.
610 10 $aUnited States. $bArmy. $bCavalry $xHistory $yCivil War, 1861-1865 $vMaps.
610 20 $aUnited Nations $zAfrica.

611 SUBJECT ADDED ENTRY - MEETING NAME (R)

A subject added entry in which the entry element is a meeting name.

Indicators
First Type of meeting name entry element
    0   Inverted name
    1   Jurisdiction name
    2   Name in direct order
Second Subject heading system/thesaurus
    0   Library of Congress Subject Headings/LC authority files
    1   LC subject headings for children's literature
    2   Medical Subject Headings/NLM authority files
    3   National Agricultural Library subject authority file
    4   Source not specified
    5   Canadian Subject Headings/NLC authority file
    6   Repertoire des vedettes-matiere/NLC authority file

Subfield Codes
$a   Meeting name or jurisdiction name as entry element (NR)
$c   Location of meeting (NR)
$d   Date of meeting (NR)
$e   Subordinate unit (R)
$f   Date of a work (NR)
$g   Miscellaneous information (NR)
$h   Medium (NR)
$k   Form subheading (R)
$l   Language of a work (NR)
$n   Number of part/section/meeting (R)
$p   Name of part/section of a work (R)
$s   Version (NR)
$t   Title of a work (NR)
$v   Form subdivision (R)
$x   General subdivision (R)
$y   Chronological subdivision (R)
$z   Geographic subdivision (R)

Examples

611 20 $aVatican Council $n(2nd : $d1962-1965). $tDecretum de presbyterorum ministerio et vita.

611 20 $aWorld Series (Baseball) $xHistory.

611 20 $aOlympic Games $n(23rd : $d1984 : $cLos Angeles, Calif.) $vPeriodicals.

650 SUBJECT ADDED ENTRY - TOPICAL TERM (R)

A subject added entry in which the entry element is a topical term.

Indicators

First Level of subject

  # No information provided

  0 No level specified

  1 Primary

  2 Secondary

Second Subject heading system/thesaurus

  0 Library of Congress Subject Headings/LC authority files

  1 LC subject headings for children's literature

  2 Medical Subject Headings/NLM authority files

  3 National Agricultural Library subject authority file

  4 Source not specified

  5 Canadian Subject Headings/NLC authority file

  6 Repertoire des vedettes-matiere/NLC authority file

  7 Source specified in subfield $2

Subfield Codes

$a Topical term or geographic name as entry element (NR)

$b Topical term following geographic name as entry element (NR)

$c Location of event (NR)

$d Active dates (NR)

$e Relator term (NR)

$v Form subdivision (R)

$x General subdivision (R)

$y Chronological subdivision (R)

$z Geographic subdivision (R)

Examples

650 #0 $aArchitecture, Modern $y19th century.

650 00 $aFlour and feed trade $vPeriodicals.

650 #0 $aVocal music $zFrance $y18th century.

651 SUBJECT ADDED ENTRY - GEOGRAPHIC NAME (R)

A subject added entry in which the entry element is a geographic name.

Indicators

First Undefined; contains a blank (#)

Second Subject heading system/thesaurus

    0   Library of Congress Subject Headings/LC authority files

    1   LC subject headings for children's literature

    2   Medical Subject Headings/NLM authority files

    3   National Agricultural Library subject authority file

    4   Source not specified

    5   Canadian Subject Headings/NLC authority file

    6   Repertoire des vedettes-matiere/NLC authority file

Subfield Codes

$a   Geographic name (NR)

$v   Form subdivision (R)

$x   General subdivision (R)

$y   Chronological subdivision (R)

$z   Geographic subdivision (R)

Examples

651 #0 $aAmazon River.

651 #0 $aPompeii (Ancient city)

651 #0 $aRussia $xHistory $vMaps.

651 #0 $aUnited States $xBoundaries $zCanada.

700 ADDED ENTRY - PERSONAL NAME (R)

Indicators

First Type of personal name entry element

    0   Forename

    1   Surname

    3   Family name

Second Type of added entry

    #   No information provided

    2   Analytical entry

Subfield Codes

$a   Personal name (NR)

$b   Numeration (Roman numerals used in the entry element of the name) (NR)

$c   Titles and other words associated with the name (R)

$d   Dates associated with the name (NR)

$e   Relator term (R)

$f   Date of a work (NR)

$g   Miscellaneous information (NR)

$h   Medium

$k   Form subheading (R)

$l   Language of a work (NR)

$n   Number of section/part of a work (R)
$p   Name of section/part of a work (R)
$q   Qualification of name (fuller form) (NR)
$t   Title of work (NR)

Examples
700 0# $aAlexander$b1,$cEmperor of Russia.
700 1# $aLawrence, D. H. $q(David Herbert)
700 1# $aal-Shaykh, Hanan,$d1945-

710   ADDED ENTRY - CORPORATE NAME (R)

Indicators
First Type of corporate name entry element
       0   Inverted name
       1   Jurisdiction name
       2   Name in direct order
Second Type of added entry
       #   No information provided
       2   Analytical entry

Subfield Codes
$a   Corporate name or jurisdiction name as entry element (NR)
$b   Subordinate unit (R)
$c   Location of meeting (NR)
$d   Date of meeting or treaty signing (R)
$e   Relator term (R)
$f   Date of a work (NR)
$g   Miscellaneous information (NR)
$k   Form subheading (R)
$l   Language of a work (NR)
$n   Number of section/part of meeting (R)
$p   Name of section/part of meeting (R)
$t   Title of work (NR)

Examples
710 1# $aUnited States. $bDept. of Agriculture.
710 2# $aSt. James Church (Bronx, New York, N.Y.)

711   ADDED ENTRY - MEETING NAME (NR)

Indicators
First Type of meeting name entry element
       0   Inverted name
       1   Jurisdiction name
       2   Name in direct order
Second Undefined; contains a blank (#)

Subfield Codes
$a   Meeting name or jurisdiction name as entry element (NR)
$c   Location of meeting (NR)
$d   Date of meeting (R)
$e   Subordinate unit (R)
$f   Date of a work (NR)
$g   Miscellaneous information (NR)
$h   Medium (NR)
$k   Form subheading (R)
$l   Language of a work (NR)
$n   Number of section/part of meeting (R)
$p   Name of section/part of meeting (R)
$q   Name of meeting following jurisdiction name entry element (NR)
$t   Title of work

Example
711 2# $aLabour Party (Great Britain). $eConference ($n71st :$cBlackpool, Lancashire)

730 ADDED ENTRY - UNIFORM TITLE (R)
Indicators
First Nonfiling characters
       0-9 Number of nonfiling characters present
Second Type of added entry
       #   No information provided
       2   Analytical entry

Subfield Codes
$a   Uniform title (NR)
$d   Date of treaty signing (R)
$f   Date of a work (NR)
$g   Miscellaneous information (NR)
$h   Medium (NR)
$k   Form subheading (R)
$l   Language of a work (NR)
$m   Medium of performance for music (R)
$n   Number of section/part of a work (R)
$o   Arranged statement for music (NR)
$p   Name of section/part of a work (R)
$r   Key for music (NR)
$s   Version (NR)
$t   Title of a work (NR)

Examples
730 0# $aGenesis (Old Saxon poem)
730 0# $aReynard the fox.$lFrench.
730 0# $aBible.$pN.T.$pMatthew.$lEnglish.$f1976.

810   SERIES ADDED ENTRY - CORPORATE NAME (R)

Indicators

First Type of corporate name entry element

    0   Inverted name

    1   Jurisdiction name

    2   Name in direct order

Second Undefined; contains a blank (#)

Subfield Codes

$a   Corporate name or jurisdiction name as entry element (NR)

$b   Subordinate unit (R)

$c   Location of meeting (NR)

$d   Date of meeting or treaty signing (R)

$f   Date of a work (NR)

$h   Medium (NR)

$k   Form subheading (R)

$l   Language of a work (NR)

$n   Number of section/part of meeting (R)

$p   Name of section/part of meeting (R)

$t   Title of work (NR)

Example

810   2# $aJohn Bartholomew and Son. $tBartholomew world travel series ;$v10.

830   SERIES ADDED ENTRY - UNIFORM TITLE (R)

Indicators

First   Undefined; contains a blank (#)

Second Nonfiling characters

    0-9 Number of nonfiling characters present

Subfield Codes

$a   Uniform title (NR)

$d   Date of treaty signing (R)

$f   Date of a work (NR)

$h   Medium (NR)

$k   Form subheading (R)

$l   Language of a work (NR)

$m   Medium of performance for music (R)

$n   Number of section/part of a work (R)

$p   Name of section/part of a work (R)

$r   Key for music (NR)

$s   Version (NR)

$t   Title of a work (NR)

$v   Volume number/sequential designation (NR)

Example

490   1# $aPolicy series/CES ;$v1

830   #0 $aPolicy series (Centre for Environment Studies (London, England)) ;$v1

ANSWERS

EXERCISE 2.1
Standard access points for these records include titles, authors (including organizations associated with the work) and subjects, but could, for example, also include call numbers or ISBNs. The access points vary according to the system.

EXERCISE 3.1

a.   Design & details : creative ideas for styling your home / Candie Frankel, Michael Litchfield, Candace Ord Manroe. – Abridged ed. – New York : MetroBooks, 1998. – 88 p. : col. ill. ; 25 cm.
Includes index.
ISBN 1567996361.

b.   The compleat angler, or, The contemplative man's recreation / Izaak Walton. – 4th ed., much enl. – London : printed for R. Marriot, 1668. – [16], 255 p. : ill. ; 15 cm.
Dedication signed: Iz. Wa.

c.   Maria de Zayas : the dynamics of discourse / edited by Amy R. Williamsen and Judith A. Whitenack. – Madison : Fairleigh Dickinson University Press, 1995. – v, 257 p. ; 24 cm.
Includes bibliographical references and index.
ISBN 0 8386 3572 5.

d.   Genetic approaches to mental disorders/ edited by Elliot S. Gershon and C. Robert Cloninger. – 1st ed. – Washington, D.C : American Psychiatric Press, 1994. – xix, 376 p. : ill. ; 24 cm. – (American Psychopathological Association series)
Includes bibliographical references and index.
ISBN 0 880 48951 0.

(There is a specified order for notes. However, at this stage transcribe the notes in any order.)

EXERCISE 3.2

a.   Soft paths : how to enjoy the wilderness without harming it / Bruce Hampton and David Cole ; edited by Molly Absolon and Tom Reed ; line drawings by Denise Casey. – Rev. and updated. – Mechanicsburg, PA : Stackpole Books, c1995. – xvii, 222 p. : ill. ; 21 cm.
Includes bibliographical references (p. 209-220) and index.
ISBN 0811730921.

b.   International Year of Disabled Persons : the story of the U.S. Council for IYDP. – Washington, D.C. : National Organization on Disability, c1983. – 96 p. : ill. ; 26 cm.
ISBN 0 961 06280 0 : $9.50.

c.   The autobiography of a slave = Autobiografia de un esclavo / by Juan Francisco Manzano ; introduction and modernized Spanish version by Ivan A. Schulman ; translated by Evelyn Picon Garfield. – Bilingual ed. – Detroit : Wayne State University Press, c1996. – 135 p. : ill. ; 23 cm. – (Latin American literature and culture series)
Includes bibliographical references.
ISBN 0814325378 (alk. paper). – ISBN 0814325386 (pbk. : alk. paper).

EXERCISE 3.3

a.

Floortje Bellefleur vindt een poes	title proper
Cok Grashoff	first statement of responsibility
ill. door Lies Veenhoven	second statement of responsibility
9e dr.	edition statement
Alkmaar	place of publication
Kluitman	publisher
1981	date of publication
92 p.	pagination
ill.	illustration
20 cm.	dimensions
Ons genoegen	series
Leeftijd tot 9 jaar	note
ISBN 90-206-7061-1	ISBN
f.4.40	terms of availability

b.

Pjesme kroz zivot i bajke za djecu	title proper
autor svih stihova u ovoj knjizi, pjesama, crteza i fotografija je isto umjetnica Depcinski Veronika	first statement of responsibility
Prvo izdanje	edition statement
Sydney	place of publication
Depcinski	publisher
1983	date of publication
15 p.	pagination
ill.	illustration
25 cm.	dimensions
Cover title	note
ISBN 0 9588754 0 5	ISBN
$6.50 Aust.	terms of availability

EXERCISE 4.1

a. **6.1F3**

6 Chapter 6 : Sound recordings

6.1 Title and statement of responsibility area of sound recordings

6.1F Statement of responsibility of sound recordings

6.1F3 Add a word to the statement of responsibility of sound recordings if the relationship is not clear

b. **7.4F3**

7 Chapter 7 : Motion pictures and video recordings

7.4 Publication, distribution, etc., area of motion pictures and video recordings

7.4F Date of publication, distribution, etc., area of motion pictures and video recordings

7.4F3 Date of creation of unedited or unpublished film or video recordings

c. **9.5D2**

9 Chapter 9 : Computer files

9.5 Physical description area of computer files

9.5D Dimensions of the physical carrier of computer files

9.5D2 Dimensions of the physical carrier of computer files if there is more than one

d. **11.2B5**

11 Chapter 11 : Microforms

11.2 Edition area of microforms

11.2B Edition statement of microforms

11.2B5 Edition statement of microforms lacking a collective title

e. **3.3D2**

3 Chapter 3 : Cartographic materials

3.3 Mathematical data area of cartographic materials

3.3D Coordinates and equinox of cartographic materials

3.3D2 Coordinates and equinox of celestial charts

f. **8.6B1**

8 Chapter 8 : Graphic materials

8.6 Series area of graphic materials

8.6B Series statement of graphic materials

8.6B1 Transcribing the series statement of graphic materials

EXERCISE 4.2

a. 1.4F, 3.4F

b. 1.1F, 6.1F

c. 1.6B, 2.6B

d. 1.5, 8.5

e. 1.7, 9.7

EXERCISE 4.3

a. Rule A.8A: Capitalize only proper nouns and the technical terms which are usually capitalized in English.

b. Rules A.13C1 and A.13E3: no.

c. Rule A.15A1: yes.

d. Rule A.17: no.

EXERCISE 4.4

a. Rule B4.A: only *i.e. et al.* or if it appears in the prescribed source of information.

b. Rule B.9: misc.

c. Rule B4.A: no.

d. Rules B.5 and B.9: yes.

e. Rules B4.A and B.14A: title—only if it says "N.S.W." on the title page; imprint—as an addition to a place name or corporate body.

f. Rule B.14BA: yes.

g. Rule B.14A: Colorado River, Ariz.

h. Rule B.2A: no.

EXERCISE 4.5

a. Rule C.2A: John XXIII.

b. Rule C.2B1 and C.2B2: no.

EXERCISE 4.6

a.   There are several definitions for edition used to refer to different types of material.
Edition: Books, pamphlets, fascicles, single sheets, etc. All copies produced from essentially the same type image (whether by direct contact or by photographic or other methods) and issued by the same entity.

b.   Caption title. A title given at the beginning of the first page of the text, or, in the case of a musical score, immediately above the opening bars of the music.

c.   Half title. A title of a publication appearing on a leaf preceding the title page.

d.   Colophon. A statement at the end of an item giving information about one or more of the following: the title, author(s), publisher, printer, date of publication or printing. It may include other information.

e.   Kit. 1. An item containing two or more categories of material, no one of which is identifiable as the predominant constituent of the item; also designated "multimedia item". 2. A single-medium package of textual material (e.g., a "press kit". A set of printed test materials, an assemblage of printed materials published under the name "Jackdaw").

f.   Mixed responsibility. A work of mixed responsibility is one in which different persons or bodies contribute to its intellectual or artistic content by performing different kinds of activities (e.g., adapting or illustrating a work written by another person).

g.   Subtitle. Not used in *AACR2*. See Other title information.

h.   Other title information. A title borne by an item other than the title proper or parallel or series title(s); also any phrase appearing in conjunction with the title proper, etc., indicative of the character, contents, etc., of the item or the motives for, or occasion of, its production or publication.

i.   Plate. A leaf containing illustrative matter, with or without explanatory text, that does not form part of wither the preliminary or the main sequence of pages or leaves.

j.   Uniform title. 1. The particular title by which a work is to be identified for cataloging purposes. 2. The particular title used to distinguish the heading for a work from the heading for a different work. 3. A conventional collective title used to collocate publications of an author, composer, or corporate body containing several works or extracts, etc., from several works (e.g., complete works, several works in a particular literary or musical form).

REVISION QUIZ 4.7

a.   1   Title and statement of responsibility
      2   Edition
      3   Material (or type of publication) specific details
      4   Publication, distribution, etc.
      5   Physical description
      6   Series
      7   Note
      8   Standard number and terms of availability

b.   i.   7.5 and 1.5
      ii.   3.2 (or 3.2B) and 1.2
      iii. 2.6B and 1.6B
      iv.   5.7B and 1.7B
      v.   6.1F and 1.1F

vi.   9.1B and 1.1B
vii.   8.1C1 and 1.C1

c.   Scope: .0A

d.   Elements are the distinct pieces of bibliographic information which form part of an area of description, e.g., the place of publication.

e.   Punctuation is used in the ISBD
- to show the beginning of each area
- to separate the elements within each area
- to identify particular elements by the punctuation which precede them.

f.   i.   Part I of AACR2   description of the item
      ii.   Dewey Decimal Classification schedules   classification number
      iii. Part II of AACR2   main & added entries and headings
      iv.   Library of Congress Subject Headings   subject headings.

g.   Appendix D – Glossary.

EXERCISE 5.1
a.   Fit for a king : the Elvis Presley cookbook.
b.   Elizabeth McKeon, Ralph Gevirtz & Julie Bandy.
c.   Yes.
d.   Yes.
e.   0517189178.
f.   TX715.2.S68 M34 1998.
g.   641.5975 ; 21st edition.
h.   Gramercy Books, 1998.
i.   Southern-style American cookery.
      Elvis Presley.

EXERCISE 5.2
a.   The field is repeatable. That is, you can have more than one added entry in a record.
b.   The entry element is a surname.

EXERCISE 6.1
a.   A dictionary of Inuit education / John McLaren

      245   1 2 $aA dictionary of Inuit education /$cJohn McLaren.

b.   Papua New Guinea : a political history / by James Griffin, Hank Nelson, Stewart Firth

      245   1 0 $aPapua New Guinea :$ba political history /$cby James Griffin, Hank Nelson, Stewart Firth.

c.   Stress busters [videorecording] : a dramatic presentation about stress, change, lifestyle and communication / Amanda Gore

(Note Rule 1.1F7 - omit most titles, qualifications, etc.)

245   1 0 $aStress busters$h[videorecording] :$ba dramatic presentation about stress, change, lifestyle and communication /$cAmanda Gore.

d.   Tom Lehrer in concert [sound recording] / Tom Lehrer

245   1 0 $aTom Lehrer in concert$h[sound recording] /$cTom Lehrer.

e.   The symphony. Volume two, Elgar to the present day / edited by Robert Simpson

245   0 4 $aThe symphony.$nVolume two ,$pElgar to the present day /$cedited by Robert Simpson.

EXERCISE 6.2

a.   New ed.

250       $aNew ed.

b.   Version 6.5

250       $aVersion 6.5.

c.   6th ed. / edited by Jeremy Judson … [et al.]

250       $a6^th ed. /$bedited by Jeremy Judson … [et al.]

d.   Rev. ed.

250       $aRev. ed.

EXERCISE 6.3

a.   Scale 1:190, 080. 1 in. to 3 miles.
OR
Scale 1:190, 080. (Include the second statement if you think it is more "precise"—Rule 3.3B2)

255       $aScale 1:190, 080. 1 in. to 3 miles.

b.   Vol. 1, no. 1 (Jan. 1964)-

362   0 $aVol. 1, no. 1 (Jan. 1964)-

c.   Issue 1 (Fall 1989)-

362   0 $aIssue 1 (Fall 1989)-

EXERCISE 6.4

a.   Albany, N.Y. : Forest Press, 1996

      260          $aAlbany, N.Y. :$bForest Press,$c1996.

b.   [California?] : Lay of the Land, c1996

      260          $a[California?] :$bLay of the Land,$cc1996.

c.   Danvers, Mass. : Boyd & Fraser, c1993

      260          $aDanvers, Mass. :$bBoyd & Fraser,$cc1993.

d.   Mt. Vernon, Va. : Prologic, 1985
      OR
      Mt. Vernon, Va. : Prologic in association with Longman Cheshire and Control Data, 1985

      (Rule 1.4D5 refers to "when the first and subsequently named entities are linked in a single statement".)

      260          $aMt. Vernon, Va. :$bPrologic,$c1985.

EXERCISE 6.5

a.   287 p. : 163 ill. (55 col.) ; 21 cm.

      300          $a287 p. :$b163 ill. (55 col.) ;$c21 cm.

b.   v. ; 25 cm.

      300          $a v. ;$c25 cm.

c.   6 computer disks : sd., col. ; 3 1/2 in. + 1 manual + 1 reference card

      300          $a6 computer disks :$bsd., col. ;$c3 1/2 in. +$e1 manual + 1 reference card.

d.   3 sound discs (179 min.) : digital, stereo ; 4 3/4 in. + 1 booklet

      300          $a3 sound discs (179 min.) :$bdigital, stereo ;$c4 3/4 in. +$e1 booklet.

EXERCISE 6.6

a.   The peoples of South-East Asia and the Pacific

      440   4 $aThe peoples of South-East Asia and the Pacific

b.   Pelican books ; A213

      490   0 $aPelican books ;$vA213

c.   (Background paper / Congress of the United States ; 42)

      490   1 $aBackground paper / Congress of the United States ;$v42

d.   (Groundwater research technical paper / Canadian Environmental Assessment Agency, ISSN 0404-7821 ; no. 1)
OR
(Groundwater research technical paper, ISSN 0404-7821 ; no.1)

(Rule 1.6E1 requires statements of responsibility "only if they are considered to be necessary for identification of the series".)

490 1 $aGroundwater research technical paper / Canadian Environmental Assessment Agency,$x0404-7821 ;$vno.1

EXERCISE 6.7

a.   Bibliographic references and index (or any similar note)

504           $aBibliographic references and index.

b.   Cover title: Picasso's success and failure

500           $aCover title: Picasso's success and failure.

c.   Contents: Concerto in D minor for trumpet and organ / Handel (10 min.) – Trumpet concerto in B flat major / Albinoni (8 min.) – Trumpet concerto in D major / Telemann (12 min.)

505 0 $aConcerto in D minor for trumpet and organ / Handel (10 min.) – Trumpet concerto in B flat major / Albinoni (8 min.) – Trumpet concerto in D major / Telemann (12 min.).

d.   First published: The potato guide, 1986

500           $aFirst published: The potato guide. 1986.

e.   Quarterly

310           $aQuarterly

f.   System requirements: Windows 3.1 or Windows 95; 8 Mb RAM; SVGA Monitor (640 x 480 pixels at 256 colors); CD-ROM drive (double speed)

538           $aSystem requirements: Windows 3.1 or Windows 95; 8 Mb RAM; SVGA Monitor (640 x 480 pixels at 256 colors); CD-ROM drive (double speed).

EXERCISE 6.8

a.   ISBN 0 7015 0465 X (cased). – ISBN 0 7015 0466 8 (pbk.)

020           $a070150465X (cased)
020           $a0701504668 (pbk.)

b.   ISSN 0002-9769 : $60 per year

022           $a0002-9769 :$c$60 per year

EXERCISE 7.1

You may not have exactly the same descriptions as these. Discuss any differences with a fellow student, teacher or supervisor.

a.   Split vision : the portrayal of Arabs in the American media / edited by Edmund Ghareeb. – Rev. and expanded ed. – Washington, D.C.: American-Arab Affairs Council, c1983. – vii, 248 p. ; 23 cm.
Includes bibliography and index.
ISBN 0-943182-00-x. – ISBN 0-943182-01-8 (pbk.)

(Rules include 1.0C1, 1.1B1, 2.1B1, A4A, 1.1E1, 2.1E1, 1.1F1, 2.1F1, 2.2B1, 1.4C1, 2.4C1, 1.4C3, 1.4D1, 2.4D2, 1.4D2, 1.4F1, 2.4F1, 1.5B1, 2.5B1, 2.5B2, 1.5D1, 2.5D1, 1.7B18, 2.7B18, 1.8B1, 2.8B1)

b.   Designing and writing online documentation : hypermedia for self-supporting products / William Horton. – 2nd ed. – New York : Wiley, c1994. – xxiii, 438 p. : ill. ; 28 cm. – (Wiley technical communication library)
Includes index.
ISBN 0-471-30635-5.

In Canada:
Designing and writing online documentation : hypermedia for self-supporting products / William Horton. – 2nd ed. – New York ; Toronto : Wiley, c1994. – xxiii, 438 p. : ill. ; 28 cm. – (Wiley technical communication library)
Includes index.
ISBN 0-471-30635-5.

(Rules include 1.0C1, 1.1B1, 2.1B1, 1.1E1, 2.1E1, 1.1F1, 2.1F1, 1.4C1, 2.4C1, 1.4C3, 1.4D1, 2.4D2, 1.4D2, 1.4F1, 2.4F1, 1.5B1, 2.5B1, 2.5B2, 1.5D1, 2.5D1, 1.7B18, 2.7B18, 1.8B1, 2.8B1)

c.   Cataloging and classification for library technicians / Mary Liu Kao. – New York : Haworth, c1995.
xii, 137 p. ; 22 cm. – (Cataloging & classification series ; 1)
Bibliography: p. 132-133.
Includes index.
ISBN 1-56024-345-7.

(Rules include 1.0C1, 1.1B1, 2.1B1, 1.1E1, 2.1E1, 1.1F1, 2.1F1, 1.4C1, 2.4C1, 1.4D1, 2.4D2, 1.4D2, 1.4F6, 2.4F1, 1.5B1, 2.5B1, 2.5B2, 1.5D1, 2.5D1, 1.7B18, 2.7B18, 1.8B1, 2.8B1)

From here on, the answers list only some of the rules used. You should continue to consult all the rules you need.

d.   Food and beverage management / Bernard Davis, Andrew Lockwood, Sally Stone. – 3rd ed. – Oxford, England ; Woburn, Mass. : Butterworth-Heinemann, 1998. – xviii, 392 p. : ill. ; 25 cm.
Includes bibliographical references and index.
ISBN 0 7506 3286 0.

(Rules include 2.1E1, 1.4C5)

e.   Organizational behavior / Roberta Kessler, Angelo Gammage. – [United States?] : HarperEducational, c1995. – xxix, 416 p. : ill. ; 25 cm.
Includes bibliography and index.
ISBN 0 06 312368 X.

f.   Essential computer concepts / Gary B. Shelly ... [et al.]. – 2nd ed. – Danvers, Mass. : Boyd & Fraser,
      c1993. – 256 p. : ill. (some col.) ; 24 cm. – (Shelly Cashman series)
      Includes bibliographical references and index.
      ISBN 0-87709-097-1.

      (Rules include 1.1F5, 2.5B2, 2.5C2, 2.1B1, 2.1E1, 2.1F1, B.14, 2.5D1, 2.8D1)

g.   The Oxford companion to music / by Percy A. Scholes. – 10th ed., rev. and reset / edited by John Owen
      Ward, Reprinted with corrections. – London ; Melbourne : Oxford University Press, 1972.
      xliii, 1189 p., 185 p. of plates : ill. ; 24 cm.
      ISBN 0 19 311306 6.

      (Rules include 1.2B1, 2.2B1, 1.2C1, 2.2C1, 1.2D1, 2.2D1, 1.4C5, 2.5B10)

h.   Instructional media and technologies for learning / Robert Heinich ... [et al.]. – 5th ed. – Englewood Cliffs,
      N.J. : Merrill, c1966. – 359 p. : ill. (some col.) ; 30 cm.
      Rev. ed. of: Instructional media and the new technologies of instruction / Robert Heinich, Michael Molenda,
      James D. Russell. 4th ed. c1993.
      Includes bibliographical references and index.
      ISBN 0-02-353070-7.

i.   Style manual for authors, editors and printers. – 5th ed., Reprinted with corrections. – Canberra : Australian
      Government Publishing Service, 1996.
      xi, 468 p. : ill. (some col.) ; 23 cm.
      Bibliography: p. 428-431.
      Includes index.
      ISBN 0 644 29770 0 (cased). – ISBN 0 644 29772 9 (pbk.)

      (Rules include 1.2D1, 2.2D1, 1.8B1, 2.8B1, 1.8B2)

EXERCISE 7.2

a.   020 $a094318200x
      020       $a0943182018 (pbk.)
      245   0 0 $aSplit vision :$bthe portrayal of Arabs in the American media /$cedited by Edmund Ghareeb.
      250       $aRev. and expanded ed.
      260       $aWashington, D.C.:$bAmerican-Arab Affairs Council,$cc1983.
      300       $avii, 248 p. ;$c23 cm.
      504       $aIncludes bibliography and index.

b.   020 $a0471306355
      245   1 0 $aDesigning and writing online documentation :$bhypermedia for self-supporting products
                /$cWilliam Horton.
      250       $a2nd ed.
      260       $aNew York :$bWiley,$cc1994.
      300       $axxiii, 438 p. :$bill. ;$c28 cm.
      440   0 $aWiley technical communication library
      500       $aIncludes index.

c. 020 $a1560243457
    245   1 0 $aCataloging and classification for library technicians /$cMary Liu Kao.
    260           $aNew York :$bHaworth,$cc1995.
    300           $axii, 137 p. ;$c22 cm.
    440   0 $aCataloging & classification series ;$v1
    504           $aBibliography: p. 132-133.
    500           $aIncludes index.

d. 020 $a0750632860
    245   1 0 $aFood and beverage management /$cBernard Davis, Andrew Lockwood, Sally Stone.
    250           $a3rd ed.
    260           $aOxford, England ;$aWoburn, Mass :$bButterworth-Heinemann,$c1998.
    300           $axviii, 392 p. :$bill. ;$c25 cm.
    504           $aIncludes bibliographical references and index.

e. 020 $a006312368X
    245   1 0 $aOrganizational behavior /$cRoberta Kessler, Angelo Gammage.
    260           $a[United States?] :$bHarperEducational,$cc1995.
    300           $axxix, 416 p. :$bill. ;$c25 cm.
    504           $aIncludes bibliography and index.

f. 020 $a0877090971
    245   0 0 $aEssential computer concepts /$cGary B. Shelly ... [et al.].
    250           $a2nd ed.
    260           $aDanvers, Mass. :$bBoyd & Fraser,$cc1993.
    300           $a256 p. :$bill. (some col.) ;$c24 cm.
    490   0 $aShelly Cashman series
    504           $aIncludes bibliographical references and index.

g. 020 $a0193113066
    245   1 4 $aThe Oxford companion to music /$cby Percy A. Scholes.
    250           $a10th ed., rev. and reset /$bedited by John Owen Ward, Reprinted with corrections.
    260           $aLondon ;$aMelbourne :$bOxford University Press,$c1972.
    300           $axliii, 1189 p., 185 p. of plates :$bill. ;$c24 cm.

h. 020 $a0023530707
    245   0 0 $aInstructional media and technologies for learning /$cRobert Heinich ... [et al.].
    250           $a5th ed.
    260           $aEnglewood Cliffs, N.J. :$bMerrill,$cc1966.
    300           $a359 p. :$bill. (some col.) ;$c30 cm.
    500           $a Rev. ed. of: Instructional media and the new technologies of instruction / Robert Heinich,
                  Michael Molenda, James D. Russell. 4th ed. c1993.
    504           $aIncludes bibliographical references and index.

i. 020 $a0644297700 (cased)
    020           $a0644297729 (pbk.)
    245   0 4 $aStyle manual for authors, editors and printers.
    250           $a5th ed., Reprinted with corrections.
    260           $aCanberra :$bAustralian Government Publishing Service,$c1996.
    300           $axi, 468 p. :$bill. (some col.) ;$c23 cm.
    504           $aBibliography: p. 428-431.
    500           $aIncludes index.

EXERCISE 8.1

1.   a.   Vol. 1, no. 1-
     b.   It is still published (or was when this record was created).
     c.   1963-
     d.   In the note field (if required, it is the first note of a serial).

2.   a.   Vol. 66, no. 1 (Jan. 1989)-
     b.   The title has changed, but the numbering has continued from the old title.

EXERCISE 8.2

There is no standard list of frequencies of serials, and there may be variations, e.g., biannual or twice a year.

a.   American libraries : the magazine of the American Library Association. – Vol. 1, no. 1 (Jan. 1970)-   . –
     Chicago : ALA, 1970-   .
        v. : ill., ports. ; 28 cm.
     11 nos. a year.
     ISSN 0002-9769.

   (Rules include 1.0C, 12.3B1, 12C1, 12.4F1, 12.5B1, 12.7B1, 12.7B23, 12.1B1, 12.3C4, B.15, 12.7B20)

b.   Omega : the international journal of management science. – Vol. 1, no. 1 (Feb. 1973)-   . – Oxford :
     Pergamon Press, 1973-   .
        v. : ill. ; 24 cm.
     Bimonthly.
     ISSN   0305-0483.

   (Rules include 1.0C, 12.3B1, 12.3C1, 12.4F1, 12.5B1, 12.7B1, 12.8B1, 12.0B1, 12.1E1, b.9, 12.3C4, 12.4F1)

c.   Journal of contemporary African studies. – Vol. 1, no. 1 (Oct. 1981)-   . – Pretoria : Africa Institute of South
     Africa, 1981-   .
        v. ; 24 cm.
     Twice a year.

   (Rules include 1.0C, 12.3B1, 12.3C1, 1.4C6, 12.4F1, 12.5B1, 12.7B1, 12.1B1, 12.4D1, 12.5D1)

For the next record, calculate the date of the first issue, and place the information you have supplied—i.e., not on the item—in square brackets. Add a note about the issue you used.

d.   The contemporary Pacific : a journal of Island affairs. – [Vol. 1, no. 1. (Spring 1989)]-   . – [Honolulu] : Center
     for Pacific Islands Studies & University of Hawai'i Press, [1989]-   . –   v. ; 26 cm.
     Twice a year.
     Description based on: Vol. 9, no. 2.
     ISSN 1043-898X.

   (Rules include 1.0C, 12.3B1, 12C1, 12.4F1, 12.5B1, 12.7B1, 12.7B23, 12.1B1, 12.3C4, B.15, 12.7B20)

e.   Historical journal. – Issue 1 (Mar. 1968)-   . – [Newcastle, N.S.W.] : University of Newcastle, 1968-   .
        v. ; 22 cm.
     Annual.

   (Rules include 1.0C, 12.3B1, 12.3C1, 1.4C6, 12.4F1, 12.5B1, 12.7B1, 12.3A1, 12.3C4, 12.0B1, 12.5D1)

EXERCISE 8.3

a. 022 $a0002-9769
    245 o o $aAmerican libraries :$bthe magazine of the American Library Association.
    260        $aChicago :$bALA,$c1970-
    300        $a v. :$bill., ports. ;$c28 cm.
    310        $a11 nos. a year
    362 o $aVol. 1, no. 1 (Jan. 1970)-

b. 022 $a0305-0483
    245 o o $aOmega :$bthe international journal of management science.
    260        $aOxford :$bPergamon Press,$c1973-
    300        $a v. :$bill. ;$c24 cm.
    310        $aBimonthly
    362        $aVol. 1, no. 1 (Feb. 1973)-

c. 245 o o $aJournal of contemporary African studies.
    260        $aPretoria :$bAfrica Institute of South Africa,$c1981-
    300        $a v. ;$c24 cm.
    310        $aTwice a year
    362        $aVol. 1, no. 1 (Oct. 1981)-

d. 022 $a1043-898X
    245 o 4 $aThe contemporary Pacific :$ba journal of Island affairs.
    260        $a[Honolulu] :$bCenter for Pacific Islands Studies & University of Hawai'i Press,$c[1989]-
    300        $a v. ;$c26 cm.
    310        $aTwice a year.
    362 o $a[Vol. 1, no. 1. (Spring 1989)]-
    500        $aDescription based on: Vol. 9, no. 2.

e. 245 o o $aHistorical journal.
    260        $a[Newcastle, N.S.W.] :$bUniversity of Newcastle,$c1968-
    300        $a v. ;$c22 cm.
    310        $aAnnual
    362 o $aIssue 1 (Mar. 1968)-

EXERCISE 9.1

a. Japan today! [sound recording] : a Westerner's guide to the people, language and culture of Japan / Theodore F. Welch, Hiroki Kato. – Lincolnwood, Ill. : Passport Books, 1991. – 1 audiocassette (56 min.) + 1 booklet.
    In slipcase.
    ISBN 0-8442-8503-X.

b. Non je ne regrette rien [sound recording] / Edith Piaf. – S.l. : EMI, p1991.
    1 sound disc (ca. 24 min.) : digital ; 4 3/4 in.
    Compact disc.
    Contents: Non je ne regrette rien – Milord – La goualante du pauvre Jean – Bal dans ma rue – Padam padam – Mon Dieu
    EMI: 701658-2.

    (Rules include 1.0C, 1.1C1, 6.5B1, 6.5B2, 6.5C2, 6.5D2, 6.7B10, 6.7B18, 6.7B19)

c.   South East Europe [map] : Bulgaria, Greece, Hungary, Romania, Yugoslavia. – Scale [ca. 1:1,250,000]. 1 in.
      to 20 miles. – Basingstoke, Hants. : Automobile Association, [198-?]
      1 map : col. ; 52 x 136 cm. – (AA European route planning series ; no. 5)
      ISBN 0 86145 072 8.

      (Rules include 1.0C, 1.1C1, 3.3B1, 3.3B2, 3.5B1, 3.5B2, 3.5D1, 3.6B1, 3.5C3)

d.   The Norton utilities for Macintosh [computer file]. – Version 3.2. – Program. – Cupertino, Calif. : Symantec,
      c1995.
      5 computer disks : col. ; 3 1/2 in. + 1 user manual.
      System requirements: Macintosh.

      (Rules include 1.0C, 1.1C1, 9.2B1, 9.3B1, 9.4F1, 9.5B1, 9.5C1, 9.5D1, 9.5E1, 9.7B1, 9.7B19)

e.   Cane toads [videorecording] : an unnatural history / written & directed by Mark Lewis. – Australia : Film
      Australia, c1987.
      1 videocassette (ca. 46 min.) : sd., col. ; 1/2 in.
      VHS.
      Credits: Photographers, Jim Frazier, Wayne Taylor; editor, Lindsay Frazer.
      Color recording system: PAL.
      Censorship rating: Parental guidance.

      (Rules include 1.0C, 1.1C1, 7.5B1, 7.5B2, 7.5C2, 7.5C3, 7.5D3, 7.7B6, 7.7B10, 7.7B14, 7.0A1, 7.0B1, 7.0B2,
      7.1B1, 1.4C6)

EXERCISE 9.2

a.   020 $a084428503X
      245   1 0 $aJapan today!$h[sound recording] :$ba Westerner's guide to the people, language and
                   culture of Japan /$cTheodore F. Welch, Hiroki Kato.
      260          $aLincolnwood, Ill. :$bPassport Books,$c1991.
      300          $a1 audiocassette (56 min.) +$d1 booklet.
      500          $aIn slipcase.

b.   245   1 0 $aNon je ne regrette rien$h[sound recording] /$cEdith Piaf.
      260          $aS.l. :$bEMI,$cp1991.
      300          $a1 sound disc (ca. 45 min.) :$bdigital ;$c4 3/4 in.
      500          $aCompact disc.
      500          $aEMI: 701658-2.
      505   0 $a Non je ne regrette rien – Milord – La goualante du pauvre Jean – Bal dans ma rue – Padam
                   padam – Mon Dieu.

c.   020 $a0861450728
      245   0 0 $aSouth East Europe$h[map] :$bBulgaria, Greece, Hungary, Romania, Yugoslavia.
      255          $aScale [ca. 1:1,250,000]. 1 in. to 20 miles.
      260          $aBasingstoke, Hants. :$bAutomobile Association,$c[198-?]
      300          $a1 map :$bcol. ;$c52 x 136 cm.
      440   0 $aAA European route planning series ;$vno. 5

d.　245　0 4　$aThe Norton utilities for Macintosh$h[computer file].
　　250　　　$aVersion 3.2.
　　256　　　$aProgram.
　　260　　　$aCupertino, Calif. :$bSymantec,$cc1995.
　　300　　　$a5 computer disks :$bcol. ;$c3 1/2 in. +$e1 user manual.
　　538　　　$aSystem requirements: Macintosh.

e.　245　1 0　$aCane toads$h[videorecording] :$ban unnatural history /$cwritten & directed by Mark Lewis.
　　260　　　$aAustralia :$bFilm Australia,$cc1987.
　　300　　　$a1 videocassette (ca. 46 min.) :$bsd., col. ;$c1/2 in.
　　500　　　$aVHS.
　　500　　　$aColor recording system: PAL.
　　500　　　$aCensorship rating: Parental guidance.
　　508　　　$aCredits: Photographers, Jim Frazier, Wayne Taylor; editor, Lindsay Frazer.

EXERCISE 10.1
a.　Harold Larwood (Rule 21.6B1)
b.　Title (Rule 21.7B1)
c.　M. Drummond (Rule 21.6C1)
d.　Title (Rule 21.6C2)
e.　Mary Mortimer (Rule 21.4A1)
f.　Title (Rule 21.7B1)

EXERCISE 10.2
a.　Michael West (Rule 21.10A)
b.　Ludwig Goldscheider (Rule 21.17B1)
c.　Lily Rose (Rule 21.12B1)

EXERCISE 10.3
a.　Main entry: Robert Moser
　　(Rules include 21.1A1, 21.1B2, 21.4A1)

b.　Main entry: American Bar Association
　　(Rules include 21.1B2, 21.4B1)

c.　Main entry: Melissa Cranshaw OR Cleveland Museum of Art
　　(Rules include 21.1A1, 21.1B2, 21.4A1)

d.　Main entry: the Conference on Energy
　　(Rules include 21.1B2)

e.　Main entry: American Antipollution Society. Standards Committee
　　(Rules include 21.1B2, 21.4B2)

f.　Main entry : National Health Policy on Tobacco in Australia and Examples of strategies for implementation.
　　(Title)
　　(Rules include 21.1B2, 21.1B3, 21.1C1)

g.   Main entry: Ohio Section of the Anarchist Party
       (Rules include 21.1B2, 21.4B2)

h.   Main entry: Trinidad Netball Association
       (Rules include 21.1B2)

i.   Main entry: Police conduct in minority communities : an issue for your consideration (Title)
       (Rules include 21.1B2, 21.1B3, 21.1C1)

EXERCISE 10.4

a.   Main entry: John S. Herrold
       Added entries: Ruth Fairchild-Carruthers. World climate. Our changing climate

       (Rules include 21.6B2, 21.6C1, 21.30B1, 21.30J1)

b.   Main entry: Roberta Jackson Hunt
       Added entries: A bibliography on weather

       (Rules include 21.4A1, 21.30J1)

c.   Main entry: President Theodore Roosevelt
       Added entries: The message of President Theodore Roosevelt to the Congress, September 8, 1904
       Theodore Roosevelt (personal heading)

       (Rules include 21.4D1, 21.30J)

d.   Main entry: Enid McFall
       Added entries: A country adventure. Weir of Hermiston by Robert Louis Stevenson

       (Rules include 21.10A, 21.9, 21.30J1)

e.   Main entry: Marianne Moore
       Added entries: The complete poetry of Marianne Moore. Simon Suggs (?)

       (Rules include 21.4A1, 21.30J1, 21.30F1)

f.   Main entry: Aristophanes
       Added entries: The birds. Robert Minton Blake
       (Rules include 21.4A1, 21.14, 21.30J1, 21.30K1c)

g.   Main entry: Chela Ormond
       Added entries: The autobiography of Frodo. The lord of the rings by J. R. R. Tolkien

       (Rules include 21.4C1, 21.30J1, 21.30G1)

h.   Main entry: Crafts of the past
       Added entries: Louis Brogan

       (Rules include 21.6C2, 21.30A1, 21.30B1)

i. Main entry: Readings in ethics
    Added entries: Louise Allenby. Kelly Bryant. R. K. Smith
    (Rules include 21.7B1, 21.30D1, 21.30A1)

j. Main entry: Three plays by contemporary American women (Collective title)
    Added entries: Honor Moore. The abdication / Wolff, R.   The ice wolf / Kraus, J.   I lost a pair of gloves
    yesterday / Lamb, M.

    (Rules include 21.7B1, 21.30D1)

EXERCISE 10.5

a. Main entry: Elizabeth Bromham
    Added entries: Title, Series
    (Rules 21.4A1, 21.30J1, 21.30K1)

b. Main entry: S. Roberts
    Added entries: R. Cuthbert, L. Comley, Title, Series
    (Rules 21.6C1, 21.30B1, 21.30J1, 21.30K1)

c. Main entry: Clifford Warne
    Added entries: Paul White, Title
    (Rules 21.6C1, 21.30B1, 21.30J1)

d. Main entry: Title
    Added entries: Maine Environmental Education Council
    (Rule 21.1B3, 21.1C1, 21.30E1)

e. Main entry: Independent Commission Against Corruption
    Added entries: Title
    (Rules 21.1B2, 21.30B1, 21.30J1)

f. Main entry: Title
    Added entries: Nathan Wright
    (Rules 21.7B1, 21.30D1)

g. Main entry: Title
    Added entries: Donald Denoon
    (Rule 21.7B1, 21.30D1)

h. Main entry: Title
    Added entries: Denes Agay, Series. Depending on the library and the nature of the collection, it could be
    beneficial to make added entries for the major composers, though it is not strictly according to the rules,
    other than Rule 21.29D.

EXERCISE 11.2

1. a. NABAC, the Association for Bank Audit, Control and Operation. Research Institute
    b. No, only the heading in (a)
    c. NABAC Research Institute
            see (search under)
        NABAC, the Association for Bank Audit, Control and Operation. Research Institute

2.   National Food Processors Association (U.S.)
           search also under the former name
      National Canners Association

      National Canners Association
           search also under the later name
      National Food Processors Association (U.S.)

EXERCISE 11.3

a.   Blythe, William Jefferson, 1946-
           search under (see)
      Clinton, Bill, 1946-

b.   Arkansas. Governor (1983-1992 : Clinton)
           search also under (see also)
      Clinton, Bill, 1946-

c.   United States. President (1993- : Clinton)
           search also under (see also)
      Clinton, Bill, 1946-

EXERCISE 12.1

a.   Fitzgerald, F. Scott (Francis Scott), 1896-1940

b.   Leong, Ka Tai

c.   Brown, Samuel Raymond, 1918-

d.   Escrivá de Balaguer, José María, 1902-1975

e.   Vita-Finzi, Claudio

f.   D'Alpuget, Blanche, 1944-

g.   Hankey, Maurice Pascal Alers Hankey, Baron, 1877-1963

h.   Philip II, King of Spain, 1527-1598

i.   Richardson, Henry Handel

j.   McCullers, Carson, 1917-1967

k.   Mailer, Norman

l.   De Paola, Tomie

EXERCISE 12.2

a. Twain, Mark, 1835-1910
> Refer from: Clemens, Samuel Langhorne, 1835-1910

b. Henríquez Ureña, Pedro, 1884-1946
> Refer from: Ureña, Pedro Henríquez, 1884-1946

c. Rawlings, Marjorie Kinnan, 1896-1953
> Refer from: Baskin, Marjorie Kinnan, 1896-1953

d. John XXIII, Pope, 1881-1963
> Refer from: Roncalli, Angelo Giuseppi, Cardinal, 1881-1963

e. Atwood, Margaret Eleanor, 1939-
> Refer from: Atwood, Margaret, 1939-

f. West, Rebecca, Dame, 1892-
> Refer from: Fairfield, Cecily Isabel, 1892-
> Andrews, Cecily Fairfield, 1892-

g. Shaw, Bernard, 1856-1950
> Refer from: Shaw, G. B. (George Bernard), 1856-1950
> Shaw, G. Bernard (George Bernard), 1856-1950

h. Kazantzakis, Nikos, 1883-1957
> Refer from: Kazan, Nicholas, 1883-1957
> Kasantzakis, Nikos, 1883-1957
> Kazandzakisz, Nikosz, 1883-1957

i. Poe, Edgar Allan, 1809-1849
> Refer from: Poe, E. A. (Edgar Allan), 1809-1849

j. Warren, Robert Penn, 1905-
> Refer from: Red, 1905-

EXERCISE 12.3

a. 100   1 $aFitzgerald, F. Scott$q(Francis Scott),$d1896-1940.

b. 100   1 $aLeong, Ka Tai.

c. 100   1 $aBrown, Samuel Raymond,$d1918-

d. 100   1 $aEscrivá de Balaguer, Jose Maria,$d1902-1975.

e. 100   1 $aVita-Finzi, Claudio.

EXERCISE 12.4

a. 700   1 $aD'Alpuget, Blanche,$d1944-

b. 700   1 $aMcCullers, Carson,$d1917-1967.

c.   700 0 $aPhilip$bII,$cKing of Spain$d1527-1598.

d.   700 1 $aRichardson, Henry Handel.

e.   700 1 $aHankey, Maurice Pascal Alers Hankey,$cBaron,$d1877-1963.

EXERCISE 12.5

These answers only provide the rules for determining access points.

7.b.   Horton, William K. (William Kendall)
Designing and writing online documentation : hypermedia for self-supporting products / William Horton. –
2nd ed. – New York : Wiley, c1994. – xxiii, 438 p. : ill. ; 28 cm. – (Wiley technical communication library)
Includes index.
ISBN 0-471-30635-5.
I. Title. II. Series.

(Rules include 21.4A1, 21.30J1, 21.30K1)

020		$a0471306355
100	1	$a Horton, William K.$q(William Kendall)
245	1 0	$aDesigning and writing online documentation :$bhypermedia for self-supporting products /$cWilliam Horton.
250		$a2nd ed.
260		$aNew York :$bWiley,$cc1994.
300		$axxiii, 438 p. :$bill. ;$c28 cm.
440	0	$aWiley technical communication library
500		$aIncludes index.

7.c.   Kao, Mary Liu
Cataloging and classification for library technicians / Mary Liu Kao. – New York : Haworth, c1995.
xii, 137 p. ; 22 cm. – (Cataloging & classification series ; 1)
Bibliography: p. 132-133.
Includes index.
ISBN 1-56024-345-7.
I. Title II. Series

(Rules include 21.4A1, 21.30J1, 21.30K1)

020		$a1560243457
100	1	$aKao, Mary Liu.
245	1 0	$aCataloging and classification for library technicians /$cMary Liu Kao.
260		$aNew York :$bHaworth,$cc1995.
300		$axii, 137 p. ;$c22 cm.
440	0	$aCataloging & classification series ;$v1
504		$aBibliography: p. 132-133.
500		$aIncludes index.

7.d. Davis, Bernard
      Food and beverage management / Bernard Davis, Andrew Lockwood, Sally Stone. – 3rd ed. – Oxford,
      [England] ; Woburn, Mass. : Butterworth-Heinemann, 1998. – xviii, 392 p. : ill. ; 25 cm.
      Includes bibliographical references and index.
      ISBN 0 7506 3286 0.
      I. Lockwood, Andrew. II. Stone, Sally. III. Title.

      020          $a0750632860
      100   1 $aDavis, Bernard.
      245   1 0 $aFood and beverage management /$cBernard Davis, Andrew Lockwood, Sally Stone.
      250          $a3rd ed.
      260          $aOxford, [England] ;$aWoburn, Mass :$bButterworth-Heinemann,$c1998.
      300          $axviii, 392 p. :$bill. ;$c25 cm.
      504          $aIncludes bibliographical references and index.
      700   1 $aLockwood, Andrew.
      700   1 $aStone, Sally.

7.e. Kessler, Roberta
      Organizational behavior / Roberta Kessler, Angelo Gammage. – [United States?] : HarperEducational,
      c1995. – xxix, 416 p. : ill. ; 25 cm.
      Includes bibliography and index.
      ISBN 0 06 312368 X.
      I. Gammage, Angelo. II. Title.

      020          $a006312368X
      100   1 $aKessler, Roberta.
      245   10 $aOrganizational behavior /$cRoberta Kessler, Angelo Gammage.
      260          $a[United States?] :$bHarperEducational,$cc1995.
      300          $axxix, 416 p. :$bill. ;$c25 cm.
      504          $aIncludes bibliography and index.
      700   1 $aGammage, Angelo.

7.f. Essential computer concepts / Gary B. Shelly ... [et al.]. – 2nd ed. – Danvers, Mass. : Boyd & Fraser,
      c1993. – 256 p. : ill. (some col.) ; 24 cm. – (Shelly Cashman series)
      Includes bibliographical references and index.
      ISBN 0-87709-097-1.
      I. Shelly, Gary B.

      (Rules include 21.6C2)

      020          $a0877090971
      245   0 0 $aEssential computer concepts /$cGary B. Shelly ... [et al.].
      250          $a2nd ed.
      260          $aDanvers, Mass. :$bBoyd & Fraser,$cc1993.
      300          $a256 p. :$bill. (some col.) ;$c24 cm.
      490   0 $aShelly Cashman series
      504          $aIncludes bibliographical references and index.
      700   1 $aShelly, Gary B.

7.g.   Scholes, Percy A.
        The Oxford companion to music / by Percy A. Scholes. – 10th ed., rev. and reset / edited by John Owen
        Ward, Reprinted with corrections. – London ; Melbourne : Oxford University Press, 1972.
        xliii, 1189 p., 185 p. of plates : ill. ; 24 cm.
        ISBN 0 19 311306 6.
        I. Ward, John Owen. II. Title

        (Rules include 21.4A1, 21.30D1, 21.30J1)

020			$a0193113066
100	1		$aScholes, Percy A.
245	1	4	$aThe Oxford companion to music /$cby Percy A. Scholes.
250			$a10th ed., rev. and reset /$bedited by John Owen Ward, Reprinted with corrections.
260			$aLondon ;$aMelbourne :$bOxford University Press,$c1972.
300			$axliii, 1189 p., 185 p. of plates :$bill. ;$c24 cm.
700	1		$aWard, John Owen.

7.h.   Instructional media and technologies for learning / Robert Heinich ... [et al.]. – 5th ed. – Englewood Cliffs,
        N.J. : Merrill, c1966. – 359 p. : ill. (some col.) ; 30 cm.
        Rev. ed. of: Instructional media and the new technologies of instruction / Robert Heinich, Michael Molenda,
        James D. Russell. 4th ed. c1993.
        Includes bibliographical references and index.
        ISBN 0-02-353070-7.
        I. Heinich, Robert. II.Heinich, Robert. Instructional media and the new technologies of instruction.

        (Rules include 21.6C2)

020		$a0023530707
245	0 0	$aInstructional media and technologies for learning /$cRobert Heinich ... [et al.].
250		$a5th ed.
260		$aEnglewood Cliffs, N.J. :$bMerrill,$cc1966.
300		$a359 p. :$bill. (some col.) ;$c30 cm.
500		$aRev. ed. of: Instructional media and the new technologies of instruction / Robert Heinich, Michael Molenda, James D. Russell. 4th ed. c1993.
504		$aIncludes bibliographical references and index.
700	1	$aHeinich, Robert.
700	1	$aHeinich, Robert.$tInstructional media and the new technologies of instruction.

9.a.   Welch, Theodore F.
        Japan today! [sound recording] : a Westerner's guide to the people, language and culture of Japan /
        Theodore F. Welch, Hiroki Kato. – Lincolnwood, Ill. : Passport Books, 1991. – 1 audiocassette (56 min.) + 1
        booklet.
        In slipcase.
        ISBN 0-8442-8503-X.
        I. Kato, Hiroki. II. Title.

020			$a084428503X
100	1		$aWelch, Theodore F.
245	1	0	$aJapan today!$h[sound recording]:$ba Westerner's guide to the people, language and culture of Japan /$cTheodore F. Welch, Hiroki Kato.
260			$aLincolnwood, Ill. :$bPassport Books,$c1991.
300			$a1 audiocassette (56 min.) +$d1 booklet.
500			$aIn slipcase.
700	1		$a Kato, Hiroki.

9.b. Piaf, Edith, 1915-1963
Non je ne regrette rien [sound recording] / Edith Piaf. – S.l. : EMI, p1991.
1 sound disc (ca. 24 min.) : digital ; 4 3/4 in.
Compact disc.
Contents: Non je ne regrette rien – Milord – La goualante du pauvre Jean – Bal dans ma rue – Padam padam – Mon Dieu
EMI: 701658-2.
I. Title.

245	1	0	$aNon je ne regrette rien$h[sound recording] /$cEdith Piaf.
260			$aS.l. :$bEMI,$cp1991.
300			$a1 sound disc (ca. 45 min.) :$bdigital ;$c4 3/4 in.
500			$aCompact disc.
500			$aEMI: 701658-2.
505	0		$aNon je ne regrette rien – Milord – La goualante du pauvre Jean – Bal dans ma rue – Padam padam – Mon Dieu.

9.e. Lewis, Mark
Cane toads [videorecording] : an unnatural history / written & directed by Mark Lewis. – Australia : Film Australia, c1987.
1 videocassette (ca. 46 min.) : sd., col. ; 1/2 in.
VHS.
Credits: Photographers, Jim Frazier, Wayne Taylor; editor, Lindsay Frazer.
Color recording system: PAL.
Censorship rating: Parental guidance.
I. Frazier, Jim. II. Taylor, Wayne. III. Frazer, Lindsay. IV. Title

100	1		$aLewis, Mark.
245	1	0	$aCane toads$h[videorecording] :$ban unnatural history /$cwritten & directed by Mark Lewis.
260			$aAustralia :$bFilm Australia,$cc1987.
300			$a1 videocassette (ca. 46 min.) :$bsd., col. ;$c1/2 in.
500			$aVHS.
500			$aColor recording system: PAL.
500			$aCensorship rating: Parental guidance.
508			$aCredits: Photographers, Jim Frazier, Wayne Taylor; editor, Lindsay Frazer.
700	1		$aFrazier, Jim.
700	1		$aTaylor, Wayne.
700	1		$aFrazer, Lindsay.

EXERCISE 13.1

a. Washington (D.C.)

b. Washington (State)

c. Mt. Pleasant (Tex.)

d. Vancouver Island (B.C.)

e. Antarctica

f. Addis Ababa (Ethiopia)

g. New York (N.Y.)

h. New York (State)

i. Acadia National Park (Me.)

j. Montréal (Québec)

k. Ayrshire (Scotland)

l. East Pakistan (Pakistan)
        see also later heading
                Bangladesh

    Bangladesh
        see also former heading
                East Pakistan (Pakistan)

EXERCISE 14.1

a. Imperial Chemical Industries Ltd.
b. Music Educators National Conference (U.S.)
c. Duke University
d. Missouri. Clean Water Commission
e. Laos
f. UNICEF
g. Native Plant Society of Oregon
h. National Underwriter Company. Reference Book Division
i. New York Times Company
j. Australian (Newspaper)

EXERCISE 14.2

a. United States. Dept. of Housing and Urban Development
b. American Stock Exchange. Market Research Dept.
c. National Clearinghouse for Family Planning Information (United States)
    Also Family Life Information Exchange (United States)
d. New York. Bureau of Vocational Information
e. Université Pierre et Marie Curie. Faculté de médecine Saint-Antoine
f. Imperial Chemical Industries Ltd. Organics Division
g. Great Britain. Ministry of Agriculture, Fisheries and Food
h. National Computer Security Center (United States)
    Also Computer Security Center (United States)
i. United States. Interstate Commerce Commission. Section of Energy and Environment
j. Mississippi. Dept. of Natural Resources
    Also Mississippi. Dept. of Environmental Quality

EXERCISE 14.3

Here are some examples, so that you can compare the structure of the headings you have found.

a. Heading: Canada Institute for Scientific and Technical Information
    Refer from: National Research Council of Canada. Canada Institute for Scientific and Technical Information

b. Heading: American Stock Exchange. Market Research Dept.

c. Heading: United Nations. Education Information Programmes
    Refer from: United Nations. Dept of Public Information. Education Information Programmes

d. Heading: United States. Dept. of Housing and Urban Development

e. Heading: Australian Bureau of Statistics
    Refer from: Australia. Australian Bureau of Statistics

f. Heading: United States. Flight Standards Service
    Refer from: United States. Federal Aviation Agency. Bureau of Flight Standards Service

EXERCISE 14.4

a   110 2 $aNative Plant Society of Oregon.
b. 110 1 $aMissouri.$bClean Water Commission.
c. 110 2 $aImperial Chemical Industries Ltd.$bOrganics Division.
d. 110 1 $aUnited States.$bInterstate Commerce Commission.$bSection of Energy and Environment.
e. 110 2 $aNational Computer Security Center (United States)

EXERCISE 14.5

a. 710 1 $aMississippi.$bDept. of Environmental Quality.
b. 710 1 $aGreat Britain.$bMinistry of Agriculture, Fisheries and Food.
c. 710 2 $aNational Underwriter Company.$bReference Book Division.
d. 710 2 $aLaos.
e. 710 1 $aMusic Educators National Conference (U.S.)

EXERCISE 14.6

7.a.   Split vision : the portrayal of Arabs in the American media / edited by Edmund Ghareeb. – Rev. and
        expanded ed. – Washington, D.C.: American-Arab Affairs Council, c1983. – vii, 248 p. ; 23 cm.
        Includes bibliography and index.
        ISBN 0-943182-00-x. – ISBN 0-943182-01-8 (pbk.)
        I. Ghareeb, Edmund. II. American-Arab Affairs Council.

        (Rules include 21.7B1)

020		$a094318200x
020		$a0943182018 (pbk.)
245	0 0	$aSplit vision :$bthe portrayal of Arabs in the American media /$cedited by Edmund Ghareeb.
250		$aRev. and expanded ed.
260		$aWashington, D.C.:$bAmerican-Arab Affairs Council,$cc1983.
300		$avii, 248 p. ;$c23 cm.
504		$aIncludes bibliography and index.
700	1	$aGhareeb, Edmund.
710	2	$aAmerican-Arab Affairs Council.

8.a.   American libraries : the magazine of the American Library Association. – Vol. 1, no. 1 (Jan. 1970)-   . –
        Chicago : ALA, 1970-   .
           v. : ill., ports. ; 28 cm.
        11 nos. a year.
        ISSN 0002-9769
        I. American Library Association

022		$a0002-9769
245	0 0	$aAmerican libraries :$bthe magazine of the American Library Association.
260		$aChicago :$bALA,$c1970-
300		$a v. :$bill., ports. ;$c28 cm.
310		$a11 nos. a year
362	0	$aVol. 1, no. 1 (Jan. 1970)-
710	2	$aAmerican Library Association.

8.c.   Journal of contemporary African studies. – Vol. 1, no. 1 (Oct. 1981)-   . – Pretoria : Africa Institute of South
        Africa, 1981-   .
           v. ; 24 cm.
        Twice a year.
        I. Africa Institute

245	0 0	$aJournal of contemporary African studies.
260		$aPretoria :$bAfrica Institute of South Africa,$c1981-
300		$a v. ;$c24 cm.
310		$aTwice a year
362	0	$aVol. 1, no. 1 (Oct. 1981)-
710	2	$aAfrica Institute.

8.d.   The contemporary Pacific : a journal of Island affairs. – [Vol. 1, no. 1. (Spring 1989)]-   . – [Honolulu] : Center
        for Pacific Islands Studies & University of Hawai'i Press, [1989]-   . –   v. ; 26 cm.
        Twice a year.
        Description based on: Vol. 9, no. 2.
        ISSN 1043-898X.
        I. University of Hawaii at Manoa. Center for Pacific Islands Studies.

022			$a1043-898X
245	0	4	$aThe contemporary Pacific :$ba journal of Island affairs.
260			$a[Honolulu] :$bCenter for Pacific Islands Studies & University of Hawai'i Press,$c[1989]- .
300			$a v. ;$c26 cm.
310			$aTwice a year.
362	0		$a[Vol. 1, no. 1. (Spring 1989)]-
500			$aDescription based on: Vol. 9, no. 2.
710	2		$aUniversity of Hawaii at Manoa.$bCenter for Pacific Islands Studies.

8.e.   Historical journal. – Issue 1 (Mar. 1968)-   . – [Newcastle, N.S.W.] : University of Newcastle, 1968-   .
v. ; 22 cm.
Annual.
I. University of Newcastle (N.S.W.)

245	0	0	$aHistorical journal.
260			$a[Newcastle, N.S.W.] :$bUniversity of Newcastle,$c1968-
300			$a v. ;$c22 cm.
310			$aAnnual
362	0		$aIssue 1 (Mar. 1968)-
710	2		$aUniversity of Newcastle (N.S.W.)

9.a.   Lewis, Mark
Cane toads [videorecording] : an unnatural history / written & directed by Mark Lewis. – Australia : Film
Australia, c1987.
1 videocassette (ca. 46 min.) : sd., col. ; 1/2 in.
VHS.
Credits: Photographers, Jim Frazier, Wayne Taylor; editor, Lindsay Frazer.
Color recording system: PAL.
Censorship rating: Parental guidance.
I. Frazier, Jim II. Taylor, Wayne III. Frazer, Lindsay IV. Film Australia V. Title

100	1	$aLewis, Mark.
245	1 0	$aCane toads$h[videorecording] :$ban unnatural history /$cwritten & directed by Mark Lewis.
260		$aAustralia :$bFilm Australia,$cc1987.
300		$a1 videocassette (ca. 46 min.) :$bsd., col. ;$c1/2 in.
500		$aVHS.
500		$aColor recording system: PAL.
500		$aCensorship rating: Parental guidance.
508		$aCredits: Photographers, Jim Frazier, Wayne Taylor; editor, Lindsay Frazer.
700	1	$aFrazier, Jim.
700	1	$aTaylor, Wayne.
700	1	$aFrazer, Lindsay.
710	2	$aFilm Australia.

EXERCISE 14.7

a.   Grand Canyon National Park (Ariz.)
Colorado River management plan / prepared by Grand Canyon National Park, National Park Service, U.S.
Dept. of the Interior. – [Washington, D.C.] : National Park Service, U.S. Dept. of the Interior, 1979. – 42 p. :
ill., maps ; 30 cm.
ISBN 0 644 00847 4.
I. United States. National Park Service. II. Title.

```
020              $a0644008474
110    2         $aGrand Canyon National Park (Ariz.)
245    1 0       $aColorado River management plan /$cprepared by Grand Canyon National Park, National
                 Park Service, U.S. Dept. of the Interior.
260              $a[Washington, D.C.] :$bNational Park Service, U.S. Dept. of the Interior,$c1979.
300              $a42 p. :$bill., maps ;$c30 cm.
710    1         $aUnited States.$bNational Park Service.
```

b.   Universiti Brunei Darussalam. Educational Technology Centre
     Guide to services / Educational Technology Centre, Universiti Brunei Darussalam. – Bandar Seri Begawan :
     The Centre, c1996.
     36 p. : col. ill. ; 21 cm.
     I. Title

```
110    2         $aUniversiti Brunei Darussalam.$bEducational Technology Centre.
245    1 0       $aGuide to services /$cEducational Technology Centre, Universiti Brunei Darussalam.
260              $aBandar Seri Begawan :$bThe Centre,$cc1996.
300              $a36 p. :$bcol. ill. ;$c21 cm.
```

EXERCISE 14.8

a.   American Anthropological Association. Meeting (1992 : San Francisco, Calif.)

```
111    2         $aAmerican Anthropological Association.$eMeeting ($d1992 :$cSan Francisco, Calif.)
```

b.   National Technologist Seminar (1st : 1986 : Faculty of Engineering, University of Dar es Salaam)

```
111    2         $aNational Technologist Seminar ($n1st :$d1986 :$cFaculty of Engineering, University of Dar
                 es Salaam)
```

c.   Oregon International Sculpture Symposium (1974 : Eugene, Or.)

```
111    2         $aOregon International Sculpture Symposium ($d1974 :$cEugene, Or.)
```

d.   International Forum on the Indian Ocean Region (1995 : Perth, W.A.)

```
111    2         $aInternational Forum on the Indian Ocean Region ($d1995 :$cPerth, W.A.)
```

e.   Chinese Education for the 21st Century Conference (1991 : Honolulu, Hawaii)

```
111    2         $aChinese Education for the 21st Century Conference ($d1991 :$cHonolulu, Hawaii)
```

EXERCISE 14.9

a. Conference on the Musical Theatre in America (1981 : C.W. Post Center)
Musical theatre in America : papers and proceedings of the Conference on the Musical Theatre in America /
edited by Glenn Loney ; sponsored jointly by the American Society for Theatre Research, the Sonneck
Society, and the Theatre Library Association. – Westport, Conn. : Greenwood Press, 1984. – xxi, 441 p. : ill. ;
25 cm. – (Contributions in drama and theatre studies, ISSN 0163-3821 ; no. 8)
Bibliography: p. 415-420.
Includes index.
ISBN 0 3132 3524 4
I. Loney, Glenn Meredith, 1928- . II. American Society for Theatre Research. III. Sonneck Society. IV.
Theatre Library Association.

020		$a0313235244
111	2	$aConference on the Musical Theatre in America ($d1981 :$cC.W. Post Center)
245	1 0	$aMusical theatre in America :$bpapers and proceedings of the Conference on the Musical Theatre in America /$cedited by Glenn Loney ; sponsored jointly by the American Society for Theatre Research, the Sonneck Society, and the Theatre Library Association.
260		$aWestport, Conn. :$bGreenwood Press,$c1984.
300		$axxi, 441 p. :$bill. ;$c25 cm.
490	1	$aContributions in drama and theatre studies,$x0163-3821 ;$vno. 8
504		$aBibliography: p. 415-420.
500		$aIncludes index.
700	1	$aLoney, Glenn Meredith,$d1928-
710	2	$aAmerican Society for Theatre Research.
710	2	$aSonneck Society.
710	2	$aTheatre Library Association.

b. Prospects for adult education and development in Asia and the Pacific : report of a regional seminar,
Bangkok, 24 November-4 December 1980. – Bangkok, Thailand : Unesco Regional Office for Education in
Asia and the Pacific, 1981.
69 p. ; 27 cm.
I. Unesco. Regional Office for Education in Asia and the Pacific.

245	0 0	$aProspects for adult education and development in Asia and the Pacific :$breport of a regional seminar, Bangkok, 24 November-4 December 1980.
260		$aBangkok, Thailand :$bUnesco Regional Office for Education in Asia and the Pacific,$c1981.
300		$a69 p. ;$c27 cm.
710	2	$aUnesco.$bRegional Office for Education in Asia and the Pacific.

EXERCISE 15.1

a. Ideas in architecture

b. Learning local history

c. Imprint (Sydney, N.S.W.)

d. CIRIA research report

e. Penguin poetry (But would you make an added entry?)

f. Occasional paper (Pennsylvania Ethnic Heritage Studies Center)

g.   Technical bulletin (Saskatchewan. Dept. of Tourism and Renewable Resources)

h.   Saunders, Janice S. Teach yourself to sew better

EXERCISE 15.2

a.   440   0 $aLearning local history

b.   490 0 $aPenguin poetry

c.   490 1 $aOccasional paper / Pennsylvania Ethnic Heritage Studies Center
        830   0 $aOccasional paper (Pennsylvania Ethnic Heritage Studies Center)

d.   490 1 $aTechnical bulletin / Saskatchewan. Dept. of Tourism and Renewable Resources
        830   0 $aTechnical bulletin (Saskatchewan. Dept. of Tourism and Renewable Resources)

EXERCISE 15.3

a.   Disadvantaged post-adolescents : approaches to education and rehabilitation / Reuven Kohen-Raz. – New
        York : Gordon and Breach,c1983.
        xii, 224 p. : ill. ; 24 cm. – (Special aspects of education, ISSN 0731-8413 ; v. 1)
        Bibliography: p. 202-211.
        Includes index.
        ISBN 0-677-06010-6

        100 1 $aKohen-Raz, Reuven.
        245 1 0 $aDisadvantaged post-adolescents :$bapproaches to education and rehabilitation /$cReuven
                       Kohen-Raz.
        260            $aNew York :$bGordon and Breach,$cc1983.
        300            $axii, 224 p. :$bill. ;$c24 cm.
        440   0 $aSpecial aspects of education,$x0731-8413 ;$vv. 1
        500            $aIncludes index.
        504            $aBibliography: p. 202-211.

EXERCISE 16.1

a.   Mother Goose
        130   0 $aMother Goose.

b.   Shakespeare, William, 1564-1616. Macbeth
        100 1 $aShakespeare, William,$d1564-1616.
        240 1 0 $aMacbeth

c.   Chanson de Roland. English
        130   0 $aChanson de Roland.$lEnglish.

d.   Bible. O.T. The song of Solomon. English
        130   0 $aBible.$pO.T.$pThe song of Solomon.$lEnglish.

e.   Arabian nights
        130   0 $aArabian nights.

f.   Dead Sea scrolls. English
      130   0 $aDead Sea scrolls.$lEnglish.

g.   Book of Mormon. French
      130   0 $aBook of Mormon.$lFrench.

EXERCISE 16.2

Dickinson, Emily, 1830-1886.
[Poems. Selections]
Selected poems / Emily Dickinson. – 1st U.S. ed. – New York : St. Martin's Press, 1993. – xvi, 128 p. ; 16 cm. – (Bloomsbury poetry classics)
Includes index.
ISBN 0 3120 9752 2 (hardcover).
I. Title: Selected poems. II. Series.

020              $a0312097522 (hardcover)
100   1 $aDickinson, Emily,$d1830-1886.
240   1 0 $aPoems.$kSelections
245   1 0 $aSelected poems /$cEmily Dickinson.
250              $a1st U.S. ed.
260              $aNew York :$bSt. Martin's Press,$c1993.
300              $axvi, 128 p. ;$c16 cm.
440   0 $aBloomsbury poetry classics
500              $aIncludes index.

EXERCISE 16.3

1.   Newsletter (Louisiana Historical Association)
      130   0 $aNewsletter (Louisiana Historical Association)

2.   Forum (NGO Forum on Women, Beijing '95)
      130   0 $aForum (NGO Forum on Women, Beijing '95)

3.   Bulletin (New York (State). Dept. of Labor)
      130   0 $aBulletin (New York (State). Dept. of Labor)

4.   Forum (Carlisle, Pa.)
      130   0 $aForum (Carlisle, Pa.)

5.   Newsletter (Ontario Forestry Association : 1997)
      130   0 $aNewsletter (Ontario Forestry Association : 1997)

EXERCISE 17.1

a.   Lousie - spelling
      Is it poetry or pottery?
      Is it Iowa or Ohio?
      Purvinace - spelling

b.   Chicheley or Chichley?
Is Botany—Nomenclature an appropriate heading? Do users know what "Nomenclature" means?

c.   Old copy; not *AACR2* punctuation
Edited by Sayre P. Schatz - should be part of area 1
Philadelphia, - should be Philadelphia :
vii, 363 p. 23 cm. - no punctuation
$10.00 - in wrong position
I. Schatz, Sayre P. ed. - more usual just to give name (without "ed.")

d.   The sky is yours : you and the world of flight - no statement of responsibility - must be level 1 description?
p. - how many?
Explores the many careers ... - unusual to give summary for a book
1. Aeronautics as a profession - is this too "adult" a heading for a children's book?

e.   Different publisher
The readers guide series - spelling?
Wrong size - should be 21 cm.

EXERCISE 17.2

```
                                              746.46
                                              LID

   Liddell, Jill

   The patchwork pilgrimage : how to create vibrant church decorations
   and vestments with quilting techniques / Jill Liddell ; with historical
   essays by Andrew Liddell. - New York : Viking Studio Books, c1993.
   vii, 172 p. : ill. (some col.) ; 29 cm.
   Includes bibliographical references (p. 172)
   ISBN 0525936890
   I. Liddell, Andrew  II. Title  1. Patchwork
```

```
   Liddell, Andrew                            746.46
                                              LID
   Liddell, Jill

   The patchwork pilgrimage : how to create vibrant church decorations
   and vestments with quilting techniques / Jill Liddell ; with historical
   essays by Andrew Liddell. - New York : Viking Studio Books, c1993.
   vii, 172 p. : ill. (some col.) ; 29 cm.
   Includes bibliographical references (p. 172)
   ISBN 0525936890
   I. Liddell, Andrew  II. Title  1. Patchwork
```

The patchwork pilgrimage   746.46
                                                                LID

Liddell, Jill

The patchwork pilgrimage : how to create vibrant church decorations
and vestments with quilting techniques / Jill Liddell ; with historical
essays by Andrew Liddell. - New York : Viking Studio Books, c1993.
vii, 172 p. : ill. (some col.) ; 29 cm.
Includes bibliographical references (p. 172)
ISBN 0525936890
I. Liddell, Andrew II. Title 1. Patchwork

Patchwork   746.46
                                                                LID

Liddell, Jill

The patchwork pilgrimage : how to create vibrant church decorations
and vestments with quilting techniques / Jill Liddell ; with historical
essays by Andrew Liddell. - New York : Viking Studio Books, c1993.
vii, 172 p. : ill. (some col.) ; 29 cm.
Includes bibliographical references (p. 172)
ISBN 0525936890
I. Liddell, Andrew II. Title 1. Patchwork

                                                            746.46
                                                                LID

Liddell, Jill

The patchwork pilgrimage : how to create vibrant church decorations
and vestments with quilting techniques / Jill Liddell ; with historical
essays by Andrew Liddell. - New York : Viking Studio Books, c1993.
vii, 172 p. : ill. (some col.) ; 29 cm.
Includes bibliographical references (p. 172)
ISBN 0525936890
I. Liddell, Andrew II. Title 1. Patchwork   S.L.

EXERCISE 17.3

Your answers may differ from these, as libraries vary significantly.

ACTIVITIES	Librarian	Library Technician	Clerical Assistant	P/T Help (e.g., students)
1. Establishes policies and procedures	✓	✓		
2. Supervision	✓	✓	(✓)	
3. Does original cataloging	✓	(✓)		
4. Performs bibliographic checking for main entries		✓	✓	✓
5. Solves difficult bibliographic checking problems	✓	✓		
6. Catalogs material with cataloging information available		✓	✓	
7. Locates records in computer-based network	✓	✓	✓	✓
8. Does descriptive and subject cataloging on problem material	✓	(✓)		
9. Checks cataloging	✓			
10. Catalogs by comparing with existing catalog records		✓	✓	
11. Checks cataloging using existing catalog records	✓	✓		
12. Enters cataloging data		✓	✓	✓
13. Checks entry of cataloging data	✓	✓		
14. Reproduces shelf list cards			✓	✓
15. Files in shelf list		✓	✓	✓
16. Checks shelf list filing	✓	✓		
17. Supervises data entry and regulates workload	✓	✓		
18. Prepares books for circulation		✓	✓	✓
19. Supervises book preparation	✓	✓		
20. Maintains authority files	✓	✓		

REVISION QUIZ 17.4

a.   Physical forms include:
- book
- card
- microfiche
- CD-ROM
- online
- computer printout.

b.   Online catalogs give users more access—by keyword, ISBN, call no., etc. But they may need help to learn how to use them.

Books, printouts, etc., are easy to scan, but very difficult to keep updated.

CD-ROMs offer the same access as OPACs, but are difficult to keep updated.

Cards are familiar to older users, but offer less access than computer catalogs.

c.   Can be searched using keywords—not just titles and subject headings
- Can be limited—by date of publication, type of material, etc.
- Can take the user to catalogs of other libraries, other databases, etc.

d.   Original cataloging is cataloging from scratch, using all the appropriate cataloging tools—AACR2, DDC or LCC, LSCH, etc.
Copy cataloging is using another record as the basis, and checking using cataloging tools.

e.   Centralized cataloging is cataloging all copies in a central location, and sending cataloged items to other locations, e.g., a public library system where the main library does all the cataloging for the branches.

f.
- cheaper and quicker—cataloging is only done once per title however many copies are bought
- consistency and high standards—fewer specialist cataloging staff
- cataloging staff builds up more expertise
- fewer sets of cataloging tools needed (they are expensive)
- end processing can also be centralized

g.
- de-skilling of other library staff
- local branches have no control over the subject headings, etc.—more difficult to relate cataloging to needs of users
- other staff have fewer tasks to share around—risk of professional staff being bored

h.
- sharing ideas, skills, work
- consistency among members of the network
- knowledge of what other libraries in the network collect
- possibility of sharing professional expertise
- awareness of scrutiny of other professionals may help keep standards high
- savings of time and effort

i.
- may take longer if a library waits for another library to catalog an item
- standards may not be consistent
- required levels of cataloging may not match

j.
- copy catalog from a network
- buy records from a supplier when you buy the items
- use CIP
- join a network and share records

k.
- locate records for copy cataloging
- verify new headings
- copy catalog
- file in shelf list
- enter data onto the system
- check and update new headings
- supervise data entry
- maintain authority file
- end processing

l. Reader services
Technical services

m. Cataloging is part of technical services.

n. The catalog is produced and maintained by technical services staff. Reader services staff use and help clients to use the catalog to locate information.

o.
- Many items may be out on loan, being used in the library or waiting to be re-shelved.
- Different formats may be shelved in different areas of the library.
- Many items cover more than one subject, or one subject from several aspects, and all items on a subject may not have the same classsification number.

p. A union catalog records the holdings of more than one library. It enables clients and library staff to know what other libraries hold, so that they can borrow from them.

q.
- decide to buy the book
- place the order
- receive the book
- record its receipt in the on-order file
- check the book and mark it with the library's ownership stamp, accession number, etc.
- mark the receipt to be paid
- catalog and classify the book
- allocate a book number
- enter the cataloging data into the system
- mark the book with the call number
- reinforce, cover, etc.
- display / shelve the new book

r. Understanding the headings in the catalog helps readers advisors to find items in the collection.
Knowing about bibliographic elements helps acquisitions staff to verify and record details correctly.

GLOSSARY

AACR *See* Anglo-American cataloguing rules

accession record A record with details of the ordering and receipt of an item in a library

access point A heading given to a catalog or database record or entry in a bibliography which enables a user to find the item

acronym A word formed from the initials of the name of an organization, system or service

adaptation A modification of a work, to suit a different group of readers, or in a different literary form or medium

added entry Any entry, other than the main entry (and subject entries), which represents the item in the catalog

alphabetic designation Numbering system for serials using letters rather than numbers, e.g., Part A, Part B, Part C

alternative title The second part of a title proper consisting of two parts; the parts are joined by the word "or", e.g., As You Like It, or, What You Will

analytical title added entry A title added entry for part of a work

analytical title page Title page of an individual monograph which is part of a series

Anglo-American cataloguing rules A set of rules for descriptive cataloging developed by the Library Association (Great Britain) and the American Library Association and published in 1967 in separate British and North American texts. Revised into one consolidated text in 1978 (Anglo-American cataloguing rules second edition—AACR2). Adopted by major libraries in most English-speaking countries and translated into many other languages

Anglo-American cataloguing rules second edition AACR2. Revision into one consolidated text in 1978 of the Anglo-American cataloguing rules

Anglo-American cataloguing rules second edition 1988 revision AACR2R. Revision in 1988 of the Anglo-American cataloguing rules second edition

Anglo-American cataloguing rules second edition 1998 revision AACR2R. Revision in 1998 of the Anglo-American cataloguing rules second edition

annual A serial published once a year

annual report An official publication reviewing the activities of an organization for one year

anonymous Of unknown authorship

anthology A collection of works or extracts of works by different authors

arabic numeral A number like 1, 2, 3 ...

area of description A major section of the bibliographic description, dealing with a particular category, e.g., publication details

artefact An object made by a person

atlas A volume of maps or charts with or without explanations

author The person chiefly responsible for the intellectual or artistic content of a work, e.g., writer of a book, compiler of a bibliography, composer of a musical work, artist, photographer

author number *See* book number

authority control The control of access points by establishing and using consistent headings

authority file A collection of authority records containing the preferred forms of headings for names, series and subjects. It can be on cards, microfiche or online

authority record A record of the preferred heading for a person, place, corporate body, series or title

authority work The establishment and maintenance of authority files

bi-annual Issued twice a year

bibliographic Related to books or other library materials

bibliographic control The creation, organization, and management of records to describe items held in libraries or databases, and to facilitate user access to those items

bibliographic description Description of an item by title, statement of responsibility, edition, date, publishing information, etc.

bibliographic identity A name under which a person writes a particular kind of material

bibliographic level 1. Complexity of bibliographic description of an item being cataloged. 2. Byte 7 of the MARC leader. The most common values are "m" for monograph and "s" for serial

bibliographic record A catalog entry in card, microtext, machine-readable or other form containing full cataloging information for a given item

biennial Issued every two years

blurb Description of a book by the publisher, usually found on the back cover or book jacket

BNB *See* British National Bibliography

book A written or printed work on consecutive sheets fastened or bound together

book catalog A catalog printed and bound in book format

book number The numbers, letters or combination of numbers and letters used to distinguish an individual item from other items with the same classification number

British National Bibliography BNB. A listing of new British publications received by the Copyright Office of the British Library and other British copyright libraries, including full cataloging data

capitalize To transcribe the first letter of a word as a capital or upper case letter

caption A heading or title of a chapter, article or page

caption title A title given at the beginning of the first page of text

card catalog A catalog whose entries are on standard 7.5 x 12.5 cm cards and filed in drawers

cartographic Representing the whole or part of the earth or any celestial body

cased *See* hard cover

catalog A list of library materials contained in a collection, a library or a group of libraries, arranged according to some definite plan

cataloger A person who prepares catalog entries and maintains a catalog so that library materials can be retrieved efficiently

cataloging The preparation of bibliographic information for catalog records. Cataloging consists of descriptive cataloging, subject cataloging and classification

cataloging-in-publication CIP. Cataloging data produced by the national library or other agency of the country of publication, included in the work when it is published

cataloging source The agency which creates and/or modifies a MARC record

cataloging tools Publications of the international cataloging rules and standards, including *Anglo-American cataloguing rules (AACR), Library of Congress subject headings (LCSH), Library of Congress classification (LCC), Dewey decimal classification (DDC)*

CD *See* compact disc

CD-ROM Compact disc read-only memory. A computer disc on which data is recorded by a laser burning millions of minute pits into the surface, and covered with a protective coating. The disc is played by a laser beam, which reads the pits and converts them into readable text and images. CD-ROM discs provide very large storage for computer programs and data, including audio, video and graphics

centralized cataloging The cataloging of library materials for more than one library (branch, etc.) carried out by a single central cataloging section

cessation The termination of publication of a serial

chart 1. A map for navigation. 2. A poster containing factual information

chronological designation Numbering of serials in date order, e.g., January 1991

CIP *See* cataloging-in-publication

classified catalog A catalog in which the entries are arranged in order of classification number

code (n) A symbol used to designate a particular data element. (v) To express in a form which the computer can use to retrieve the information

collation The physical description of an item, including number of pages, illustrations, size, etc.

collective biography Stories of the lives of a number of people

collective title The title of an item containing several works

colophon A statement at the end of an item giving information about title, author, publisher, etc.

compact disc CD. A sound disc on which sound is recorded by a laser burning millions of minute pits into the surface, and covered with a protective coating. The disc is played by a laser beam, which reads the pits and converts them into sound

compact disc read-only memory *See* CD-ROM

compilation A work created by assembling material from other books

compiler 1. A person who selects and puts together material written by other people. 2. A person who writes a reference work made up of many different entries, e.g., a dictionary

compound surname A surname consisting of two or more proper names, sometimes connected by a hyphen or conjunction and/or preposition

conference proceedings The published papers given at a conference

content The bibliographic information contained in the MARC record

content designation In MARC, all the tags, indicators and subfield codes which identify elements of the content of a record

content designator In MARC, a tag, indicator or subfield code which designates an element of the content of a record

control field A field in a MARC record with a tag 001-009 and no indicators or subfield codes. Control fields contain coded data used in processing the record

cooperative cataloging Sharing of catalog records by participating libraries

copy cataloging The process of copying cataloging details from an existing catalog record and adding local location and holdings details

copyright date The date identified in a work by the symbol ©

corporate body An organization or group of people identified by a particular name and acting as an entity

data element A single piece of information, e.g., date of publication

data element identifier The lowercase letter which identifies a data element in a subfield

data field A field in a machine-readable record used to store data

date of publication The earliest year in which the particular edition of the work was published, e.g., if a second edition was published in 1991, and reprinted without alteration in 1993, the date of publication of this edition is 1991

delete To remove from a database, the MARC format, etc.

delimiter A symbol used to introduce a new subfield or to indicate the end of a field; it can vary according to the system

description Information about a work which can be derived from the work itself, including title, statement of responsibility, edition, publication details, physical description, series and ISBN

descriptive cataloging The process which describes an item and identifies and formats access points

dictionary catalog A catalog with all the entries arranged in a single alphabetical sequence

dimensions Size

display constant Word or words which precede some data when it is displayed, which are not entered in the MARC record, e.g., Summary:

dissertation A treatise prepared for the award of a diploma or degree, especially a postgraduate degree

distribution Transporting, marketing, merchandising and selling an item

distributor An agent which has marketing rights for an item

divided catalog A catalog in which the entries are divided into separate sequences, usually author-title and subject entries

edition All the copies of a work produced from the same original

edition statement The part of the description which indicates the particular edition of the work, e.g., revised, illustrated, student, abridged

editor Person who prepares another person's work for publication

e-journal A periodical published in electronic format and made available via the Internet

element A distinct piece of bibliographic information which forms part of an area of description

end matter The material at the end of a work, following the text, e.g., appendices, index, etc.

entry element Part of the name under which the name will be found in a catalog or bibliography

explanatory reference A longer "see" or "see also" reference which explains when a heading or headings should be used

extent of item Number and specific material designation of the parts of the item being described

facsimile An exact copy

family name The hereditary surname of a family

festschrift A publication in honor of a person

field Unit of information in a MARC record which corresponds to an area of description or other piece of information, e.g., access point

file characteristics Type and number of records, etc., in a computer file

filing indicator The indicator which tells the computer how many characters to ignore when filing

fixed field data Data in a MARC record where the size of the field is predetermined

fly leaf The blank sheet at the beginning or end of a book

fly-title *See* half title

forename The name that precedes the family name or surname; a first name

foreword A brief statement of the reasons for the book, usually by the author or editor. It appears after the title page and before the introduction

format 1. Appearance and make-up of a book; its size, paper, type, binding, etc. 2. Physical type of an audiovisual item, e.g., slide, filmstrip, etc. 3. Physical organization of a catalog, e.g., card, microfiche, online, etc.

format integration Validation of all data elements for all forms of material

frequency Interval between issues of a serial, e.g., weekly, quarterly

frontispiece An illustration facing or preceding the title page

general material designation GMD. Broad category of material to which an item belongs—e.g., sound recording—defined in *AACR2*

geographic name Name of a place—country, state, city, town, suburb, etc.

GMD *See* general material designation

half title The brief title of a book which appears on the leaf preceding the title page

hardback *See* hard cover

hard bound *See* hard cover

hard cover Bound in cloth- or paper-covered boards

heading A name, word or phrase at the head of a catalog entry to provide an access point

impression All copies of an edition of a work printed at one time

imprint Publication details—place, publisher, date of publication

indicator A character which gives additional information about a field, e.g., the first indicator 1 added to the tag 245 shows that a title added entry is to be made

indicator count The number of indicators in each variable data field. In MARC records it is always 2

initial The first, uppercase letter of a word

initial article The word which introduces a noun at the beginning of a title, e.g., the, a, an, le, la, les, los

initialism *See* acronym

International Standard Bibliographic Description ISBD. Standard set of bibliographic elements in standard order and with standard punctuation, published by the International Federation of Library Associations and Institutions (IFLA)

International Standard Book Number ISBN. A number intended to be unique, assigned by an agency in each country to all books published. Identifies the publisher, language and title. Adopted internationally in 1969

International Standard Music Number ISMN. An internationally recognized number assigned to printed music by the International Standard Music Number Agency in Berlin

International Standard Serial Number ISSN. An internationally recognised number assigned to each serial publication by the International Serials Data System (ISDS), a network of national centres sponsored by Unesco

issue A single copy of a serial title

joint author A writer who collaborates with one or more others in the preparation of a work

Joint Steering Committee for the Revision of AACR JSC. The committee consisting of representatives of the American Library Association, the Australian Committee on Cataloguing, the British Library, the Canadian Committee on Cataloguing, the Library Association and the Library of Congress, established to review, advise on and promote the *Anglo-American cataloguing rules*

journal A periodical issued by an institution, corporation or learned society containing current information and reports of activities or works in a particular field

JSC *See* Joint Steering Committee for the Revision of AACR

key-title The unique name given to a serial by the International Serials Data System (ISDS)

kit An item containing more than one kind of material, none of which is predominant, e.g., a set of slides and an audiocassette

LCMARC Library of Congress machine-readable cataloging format

leader Top line of a MARC record which gives information about the record to the computer program which processes it

leaf A sheet of paper consisting of two pages, one on each side

legend Bytes 6-9 of the MARC leader

logical record length The length of a self-contained MARC record

machine-readable Needing a computer to process or interpret

Machine-Readable Bibliographic Information Committee *See* MARBI

machine-readable cataloging *See* MARC

main entry The principal entry in a catalog which contains the complete record of an item

manuscript A hand-written or typescript document

map A representation, normally to scale, of an area of the earth's surface or another celestial body

MARBI Machine-Readable Bibliographic Information Committee. North American committee which revises and develops the MARC format

MARC Machine readable cataloging. A system developed by the Library of Congress in 1966 so that libraries can share machine-readable bibliographic data

mark of omission Punctuation mark showing something has been left out ...

masthead Statement of title, ownership, editors, etc., of a newspaper or periodical

mathematical data Information for maps including statements of scale, projection, coordinates and equinox

mixed responsibility Different persons or bodies make different kinds of contributions to a work, e.g., author and illustrator

modification Alteration of a work

monograph A publication either complete in one part or in a finite number of separate parts

monographic series A series of related monographs with a collective title as well as individual titles

monograph in series A monograph which is part of a series with a common series title

musical presentation statement A term or phrase indicating the physical presentation of the music, e.g., score, miniature score

name authority file A collection of authority records containing the preferred forms of headings for names, including personal and corporate names. It can be on cards, microfiche, CD-ROM or online

name-title added entry An added entry consisting of the name of a person or corporate body and the title of an item

name-title reference A reference made from the name of a person or corporate body and the title of an item

named revision A named reissue of a particular edition containing changes from that edition

national union catalog A listing of the holdings of a large number of libraries in a country

non-book material Also nonprint material. Material other than printed materials, e.g., audiovisual material, computer software

nonprint material *See* non-book material

note Descriptive information which cannot be fitted into other areas of the bibliographic description

numeric designation Numbering of a serial using numbers, e.g., Volume 1, number 1

obsolete No longer used in new or retrospective records (of a MARC content designator)

OCLC Online Computer Library Center. A bibliographic network which provides cataloging, resource sharing and reference services worldwide

online Having direct access to information stored in a computer, having interactive communication with a computer

online public access catalog OPAC. A computer-based catalog which library users access via terminals

OPAC *See* online public access catalog

optical disc A plastic disc which can be read using a light beam, including compact discs, CD-ROMs, laser dics and DVDs

original cataloging Cataloging done for the first time, using cataloging tools to create the record

other title information Title on an item other than the title proper or parallel or series title; also any phrase appearing in conjunction with the title proper

pagination The number of pages or leaves (or both) of a book identified in the bibliographic description of a book

pamphlet A small (usually less than fifty pages) printed work on a topic of current interest

parallel title Title proper in another language and/or script

periodical A serial with a distinctive title intended to appear in successive parts at stated and regular intervals. Often used as a synonym for serial

physical description Information about the physical form of an item, e.g., pagination, type of recording, dimensions

precataloging Bibliographic searching, usually done before ordering an item, to establish correct bibliographic information

preface The author's or editor's reasons for the book. It appears after the title page and before the introduction

preliminary pages The material at the beginning of a work including contents, introduction, foreword

pseudonym A fictitious name used by an author

publication The issuing of copies of a book or other item to the public

publisher A person or body which issues copies of a book or other item to the public

qualifier An addition to a name, etc., enclosed in parentheses

realia Three-dimensional objects

record status Byte 5 of the MARC leader. The most common values are "n" for new record and "c" for changed record

record structure The organization of the MARC record into the leader, the directory and the variable fields

recto The right-hand page of an open book

refer Make a reference (to)

reference A direction from one heading or entry to another

repeatable Able to be used more than once within a record

reprint A new printing of a work made from the original type face

revision A new edition of a work containing alterations and/or additions

romanization Rendering of the letters or characters of another alphabet into those of the roman alphabet

roman numeral A number like I, II, III, IV, ...

running title A title or shortened title which appears at the top or bottom of the pages of a work, usually a serial

sacred work A basic writing of a religion, such as *The Bible, Koran, Talmud,* which is generally accepted by followers of the religion

scale The ratio of distances on a map to the corresponding values on the earth

see also reference A direction from one heading to another when both are used

see reference A direction from one heading (which is not used) to another heading (which is used)

serial A publication issued in successive parts and intended to be continued indefinitely

serial issue A single copy of a serial title

serial title The title of all issues of a serial. Some serials also give titles to individual issues

series A number of works related to each other by the fact that they have a collective title, as well as each work having its own title proper

series title The collective title of a group of monographs, each of which also has an individual title

series title page An added title page bearing the series title proper

shared cataloging *See* cooperative cataloging

shared responsibility Collaboration between two or more persons or bodies performing the same function in the creation of a work

shelf list The record of the works in a library in the order in which they are shelved

specific material designation A term indicating the specific class of material—e.g., poster—to which an item belongs

spine The part of a book's cover which holds the front and back together

spine title The title on the spine of a book

standardize Make standard by applying a set of rules

standard number An ISBN, ISSN or other internationally agreed upon standard number which identifies the item uniquely

statement of responsibility A statement taken from the item which describes the person or persons or corporate body or bodies responsible for the intellectual or artistic content of the item

subfield Part of the MARC record which contains an element of description or other small piece of information

subfield code The two-character code which precedes a data element in a MARC record, e.g., $a

subfield delimiter The character used to introduce a subfield in a MARC record, e.g., $

subject cataloging Describing the content of a work using subject headings and a classification number

subject entry An entry under the heading for the subject

subject heading A heading which describes a subject and provides subject access to a catalog

subordinate body A corporate body which is part of a larger corporate body

subtitle *See* other title information

supplement 1. An item issued separately which brings a monograph up to date or otherwise adds to the work. 2. Extra issues of a serial title

tag A label which identifies each field of a MARC record, e.g., 245 identifies the title and statement of responsibility field

technical services Library services which deal with the bibliographic control—including acquisition, cataloging and end processing—of library material

terms of availability Terms on which the item is available, including price or other statement

thesis *See* dissertation

title A word or phrase which names the item

title page The page which provides the most complete information about the author and title, and is used as the most authoritative source of cataloging data

title proper The main name of an item, including alternative title(s) but excluding parallel titles and other title information

traced series A series for which an added entry is made

tracing A record of a heading under which an item is entered in a catalog

tracing note *See* tracing

transliteration Rendering of the letters or characters of one alphabet into those of another

UKMARC United Kingdom machine-readable cataloging. The machine-readable cataloging format developed by the British Library and used in the UK

uncontrolled Not verified in an authority file

uniform title 1. A title chosen to identify a monograph appearing under different titles. 2. A title used to distinguish the heading for one serial or series from the heading for another serial or series

union catalog Catalog of the holdings of more than one library

untraced series A series for which no added entry is made

USMARC US machine-readable cataloging. The machine-readable cataloging format developed by the Library of Congress and used in the United States. It is increasingly becoming the world standard for bibliographic data

validation Authorizing the use of

variable control field A field in a MARC record with a tag 001-009 and no indicators or subfield codes. Control fields contain coded data used in processing the record

variable field A field containing either control or bibliographic data

variant title A different form of the title

version A different edition, manifestation or adaptation of a work

verso The left-hand page of an open book; the back of a leaf of a book, e.g., verso of the title page

volume 1. What is contained in one binding of a monograph. 2. A number of issues of a serial, usually those published in one twelve-month period

BIBLIOGRAPHY

Anglo-American Cataloging Rules

ALCTS Interactive Multimedia Guidelines Review Task Force. *Guidelines for Bibliographic Description of Interactive Multimedia.* Chicago: ALA, 1994.

Byford, John, Keith V. Trickey, and Susi Woodhouse (eds). *AACR, DDC, MARC and Friends: the Role of CIG in Bibliographic Control.* London: Library Association, 1993.

Anglo-American Cataloguing Rules, 2nd ed., 1998 rev. Ottawa: Canadian Library Association, 1998.

Geer, Beverley and Beatrice L. Caraway. *Notes for Serials Cataloging,* 2nd ed. Englewood, Colo.: Libraries Unlimited, 1998.

Howarth, Lynne. *AACR2 Decisions and Rule Interpretations,* 6th ed. Ottawa: Canadian Library Association, 1994.

Piggott, Mary, *The Cataloger's Way through AACR2 from Document Receipt to Document Retrieval.* London: Library Association, 1990.

Smiraglia, Richard P. (ed). *Origins, Content, and Future of AACR2 Revised.* New York: American Library Association, 1992.

Smith, David. *Using the New AACR2: An Expert Systems Approach to Choice of Access Points,* rev. ed. London: Library Association, 1993.

Authority Work

Clack, Doris Hargrett. *Authority Control: Principles, Applications and Instructions.* Chicago: American Library Association, 1990.

MARC

Crawford, Walt. *MARC for Library Use: Understanding Integrated USMARC,* 2nd ed. Boston: G.K. Hall, 1989.

Multimedia Learning Resources

CatSkill, Version 2. Canberra: DocMatrix and Learning Curve, 1998.

Format integration made easy. Canberra: DocMatrix and Learning Curve, 1996.

USMARC made easy. Canberra: DocMatrix and Learning Curve, 1996.

INDEX

ABOUT THE AUTHOR

Mary Mortimer is a teacher, librarian, author, and publisher. She is a director of DocMatrix Pty Limited, and was coordinator of the Library Studies program at the Canberra Institute of Technology in Canberra, Australia. She is the coauthor of *CatSkill* (InfoTrain, 1998) and *US MARC Made Easy* (InfoTrain, 1997), which are interactive multimedia training programs for libraries, author of *Learn Dewey Decimal Classification (Edition 21)* and *LibrarySpeak* (Scarecrow, 2000), and contributor to many other publications.